JOURNEYS

Reader's Notebook

Volume 1

Kindergarten

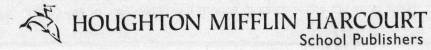

HOUGHTON MIFFLIN HARCOURT

School Publishers

Contents

Welcome to Kindergarten WTK1

Unit 1

Lesson 1: What Makes a Family? 1
Lesson 2: How Do Dinosaurs Go to School? 9
Lesson 3: Please, Puppy, Please 17
Lesson 4: Everybody Works 26
Lesson 5: The Handiest Things in the World 31

Unit 2

Lesson 6: My Five Senses 39
Lesson 7: Mice Squeak, We Speak 44
Lesson 8: Move! 49
Lesson 9: What Do Wheels Do All Day? 54
Lesson 10: Mouse Shapes 59

Contents

Unit 3

Lesson 11: Jump into January   67

Lesson 12: Snow   72

Lesson 13: What Do You Do With a Tail Like This?   77

Lesson 14: Turtle Splash!   82

Lesson 15: What a Beautiful Sky!   87

Sound/Spelling Cards   95

Letter Cards   99

High-Frequency Word Cards   101

Name _____

Aa Bb Cc Dd Ee Ff Gg Hh Ii Jj Kk Ll Mm

Nn Oo Pp Qq Rr Ss Tt Uu Vv Ww Xx Yy Zz

Aa Aa

M	x	A	b	S	a	F	l
r	A	a	C	a	T	n	A
O	z	L	a	A	i	a	A
a	J	a	A	h	A	A	a

Directions Have children identify and write uppercase *A* and lowercase *a*. Then have them circle all the *A*'s and *a*'s in the box.

Remind children to write the upper- and lowercase letters so they can be easily read, using a left-to-right and top-to-bottom progression.

Letter Names

WTK 1

Kindergarten, Welcome to Kindergarten

Name _____

Aa Bb Cc Dd Ee Ff Gg Hh Ii Jj Kk Ll Mm

Nn Oo Pp Qq Rr Ss Tt Uu Vv Ww Xx Yy Zz

Bb Bb

B	y	B	c	T	b	G	m
s	B	b	D	b	U	o	B
P	a	M	b	B	j	B	a
S	K	b	C	i	M	B	b

Directions Have children identify and write uppercase *B* and lowercase *b*. Then have them circle all the *B*'s and *b*'s in the box.

Remind children to write the upper- and lowercase letters so they can be easily read, using a left-to-right and top-to-bottom progression.

Letter Names

WTK
2

Kindergarten, Welcome to Kindergarten

Name _____

Aa Bb Cc Dd Ee Ff Gg Hh Ii Jj Kk Ll Mm

Nn Oo Pp Qq Rr Ss Tt Uu Vv Ww Xx Yy Zz

Cc Cc

O	z	C	d	U	c	H	n
t	H	c	E	c	V	p	C
Q	b	N	c	C	k	C	c
a	L	c	C	j	C	C	M

Directions Have children identify and write uppercase *C* and lowercase *c*. Then have them circle all the *C*'s and *c*'s in the box.

Remind children to write the upper- and lowercase letters so they can be easily read, using a left-to-right and top-to-bottom progression.

Kindergarten, Welcome to Kindergarten

Letter Names

Name _____

Aa Bb Cc Dd Ee Ff Gg Hh Ii Jj Kk Ll Mm

Nn Oo Pp Qq Rr Ss Tt Uu Vv Ww Xx Yy Zz

Dd Dd

P	a	D	e	V	d	I	o
u	D	d	F	d	W	q	D
R	c	O	d	D	l	D	d
d	M	d	D	k	D	D	d

Directions Have children identify and write uppercase *D* and lowercase *d*. Then have them circle all the *D*'s and *d*'s in the box.

Remind children to write the upper- and lowercase letters so they can be easily read, using a left-to-right and top-to-bottom progression.

Letter Names
© Houghton Mifflin Harcourt Publishing Company. All rights reserved.

WTK
4

Kindergarten, Welcome to Kindergarten

Name _____

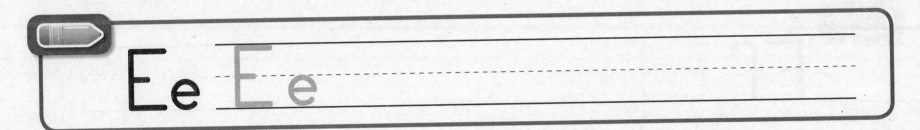

Aa Bb Cc Dd Ee Ff Gg Hh Ii Jj Kk Ll Mm

Nn Oo Pp Qq Rr Ss Tt Uu Vv Ww Xx Yy Zz

Ee Ee _____

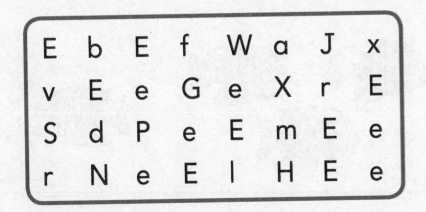

E	b	E	f	W	a	J	x
v	E	e	G	e	X	r	E
S	d	P	e	E	m	E	e
r	N	e	E	l	H	E	e

Directions Have children identify and write uppercase *E* and lowercase *e*. Then have them circle all the *E*'s and *e*'s in the box.

Remind children to write the upper- and lowercase letters so they can be easily read, using a left-to-right and top-to-bottom progression.

WTK 5

Kindergarten, Welcome to Kindergarten

Letter Names

Name _____

Aa Bb Cc Dd Ee Ff Gg Hh Ii Jj Kk Ll Mm

Nn Oo Pp Qq Rr Ss Tt Uu Vv Ww Xx Yy Zz

Ff Ff _____

R	c	F	g	X	f	K	q
w	F	f	H	f	Y	s	F
T	e	Q	f	F	n	F	f
f	O	f	F	m	F	F	f

Directions Have children identify and write uppercase *F* and lowercase *f*. Then have them circle all the *F*'s and *f*'s in the box.

Remind children to write the upper- and lowercase letters so they can be easily read, using a left-to-right and top-to-bottom progression.

Name _____

Aa Bb Cc Dd Ee Ff Gg Hh Ii Jj Kk Ll Mm

Nn Oo Pp Qq Rr Ss Tt Uu Vv Ww Xx Yy Zz

Gg Gg

S	d	V	h	Y	G	L	r
x	G	g	I	g	Z	t	B
U	f	R	g	G	o	G	g
b	P	g	T	s	G	G	g

Directions Have children identify and write uppercase *G* and lowercase *g*. Then have them circle all the *G*'s and *g*'s in the box.

Remind children to write the upper- and lowercase letters so they can be easily read, using a left-to-right and top-to-bottom progression.

Kindergarten, Welcome to Kindergarten

Letter Names

Name _____

Aa Bb Cc Dd Ee Ff Gg Hh Ii Jj Kk Ll Mm

Nn Oo Pp Qq Rr Ss Tt Uu Vv Ww Xx Yy Zz

Hh Hh

T	e	H	i	Z	h	M	s
y	H	h	J	h	A	u	H
V	g	S	h	H	p	H	h
h	Q	h	H	o	H	H	h

Directions Have children identify and write uppercase *H* and lowercase *h*. Then have them circle all the *H*'s and *h*'s in the box.

Remind children to write the upper- and lowercase letters so they can be easily read, using a left-to-right and top-to-bottom progression.

Name

Aa Bb Cc Dd Ee Ff Gg Hh Ii Jj Kk Ll Mm

Nn Oo Pp Qq Rr Ss Tt Uu Vv Ww Xx Yy Zz

Ii Ii

U	n	I	j	I	i	N	t
z	I	i	K	i	B	v	I
L	h	T	i	I	q	I	d
a	R	i	H	p	I	C	i

Directions Have children identify and write uppercase *I* and lowercase *i*. Then have them circle all the *I*'s and *i*'s in the box.

Remind children to write the upper- and lowercase letters so they can be easily read, using a left-to-right and top-to-bottom progression.

Kindergarten, Welcome to Kindergarten

Letter Names

Name _____

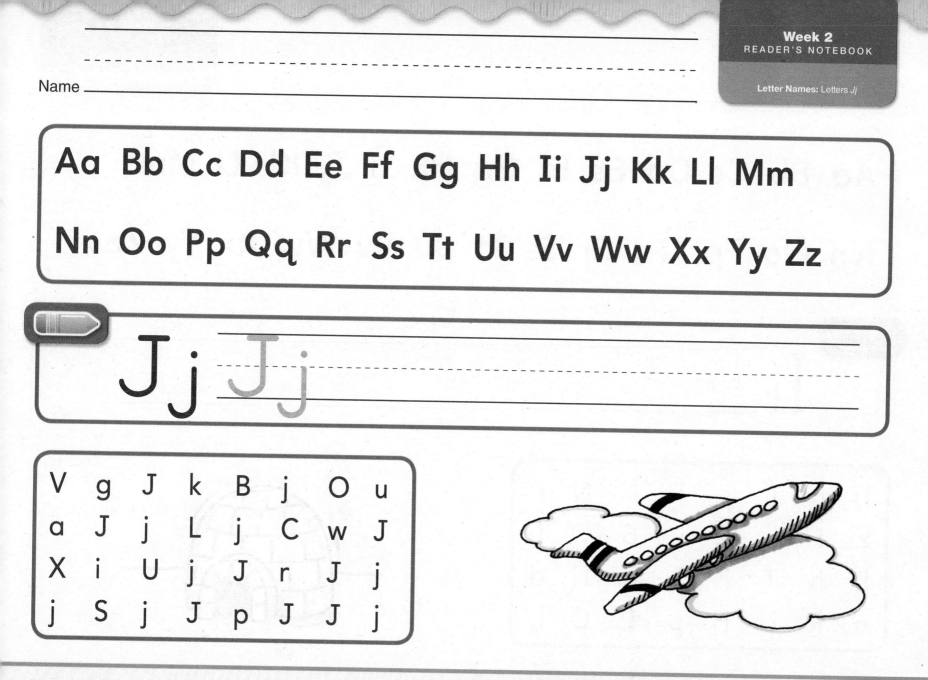

Aa Bb Cc Dd Ee Ff Gg Hh Ii Jj Kk Ll Mm

Nn Oo Pp Qq Rr Ss Tt Uu Vv Ww Xx Yy Zz

J j J j

V	g	J	k	B	j	O	u
a	J	j	L	j	C	w	J
X	i	U	j	J	r	J	j
j	S	j	J	p	J	J	j

Directions Have children identify and write uppercase *J* and lowercase *j*. Then have them circle all the *J*'s and *j*'s in the box.

Remind children to write the upper- and lowercase letters so they can be easily read, using a left-to-right and top-to-bottom progression.

Name _____

Aa Bb Cc Dd Ee Ff Gg Hh Ii Jj Kk Ll Mm

Nn Oo Pp Qq Rr Ss Tt Uu Vv Ww Xx Yy Zz

Kk Kk _____

W	h	K	l	C	k	P	v
b	K	k	M	k	E	x	K
Y	j	V	k	K	s	K	k
k	T	k	K	q	K	K	k

Directions Have children identify and write uppercase *K* and lowercase *k*. Then have them circle all the *K*'s and *k*'s in the box.

Remind children to write the upper- and lowercase letters so they can be easily read, using a left-to-right and top-to-bottom progression.

1

Letter Names

Name _____

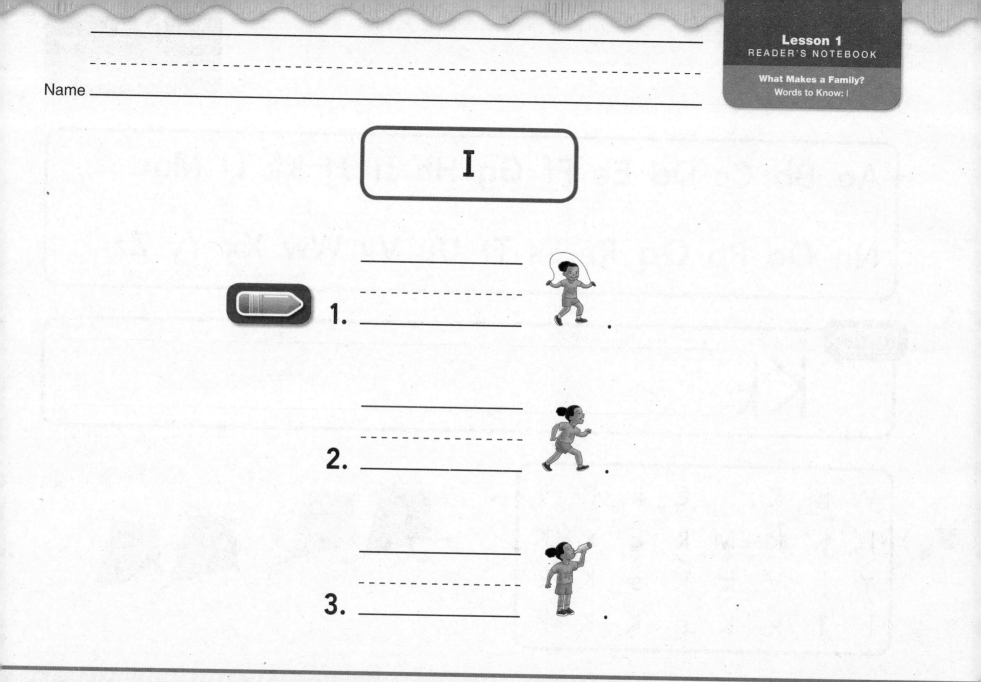

I

1.

2.

3.

Directions Have children look at each picture and name the action. Then have them write the word *I* to complete each sentence. Have children read the completed sentences aloud.

Have children tap their desks once for each word as they read the sentences aloud again. Have children say other sentences with the word *I*.

2

Name _____

Aa Bb Cc Dd Ee Ff Gg Hh Ii Jj Kk Ll Mm

Nn Oo Pp Qq Rr Ss Tt Uu Vv Ww Xx Yy Zz

Ll   Ll

X	i	L	m	D	l	Q	w
c	L	l	N	l	F	y	L
Z	k	W	l	L	t	L	Ll
l	U	l	L	r	L	L	l

Directions Have children identify and write uppercase *L* and lowercase *l*. Then have them circle all the *L*'s and *l*'s in the box.

Remind children to write the upper- and lowercase letters so they can be easily read, using a left-to-right and top-to-bottom progression.

3

Letter Names

Kindergarten, Unit 1

Name _____

Aa Bb Cc Dd Ee Ff Gg Hh Ii Jj Kk Ll Mm

Nn Oo Pp Qq Rr Ss Tt Uu Vv Ww Xx Yy Zz

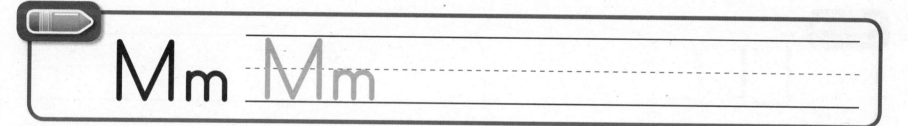

Mm Mm

Y	j	B	n	M	m	R	x
d	M	m	O	m	G	z	L
A	l	X	m	M	u	D	m
g	V	m	M	s	e	M	m

MAIL

Directions Have children identify and write uppercase *M* and lowercase *m*. Then have them circle all the *M*'s and *m*'s in the box.

Remind children to write the upper- and lowercase letters so they can be easily read, using a left-to-right and top-to-bottom progression.

Name _____

Main Ideas

Directions Tell children to draw a picture to show some important facts they learned about families from the Big Book. Have children share their pictures with the class. Tell them to speak clearly and use complete sentences as they share information.

In addition, tell them to listen carefully as others speak and to face others as they share.

Comprehension

Kindergarten, Unit 1

Name _____

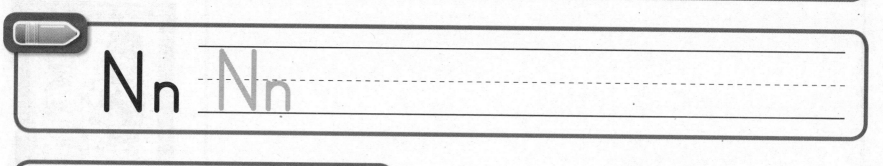

Aa Bb Cc Dd Ee Ff Gg Hh Ii Jj Kk Ll Mm

Nn Oo Pp Qq Rr Ss Tt Uu Vv Ww Xx Yy Zz

Nn *Nn*

Z	k	N	o	F	n	S	y
e	N	n	P	n	H	a	N
B	m	Y	n	N	v	N	n
n	W	n	N	t	N	N	n

Directions Have children identify and write uppercase *N* and lowercase *n*. Then have them circle all the *N*'s and *n*'s in the box.

Remind children to write the upper- and lowercase letters so they can be easily read, using a left-to-right and top-to-bottom progression.

Letter Names

Kindergarten, Unit 1

Name _____

Aa Bb Cc Dd Ee Ff Gg Hh Ii Jj Kk Ll Mm

Nn Oo Pp Qq Rr Ss Tt Uu Vv Ww Xx Yy Zz

Oo   Oo

A	l	H	o	G	p	T	z
d	O	o	Q	h	I	b	T
C	n	Z	o	O	w	O	o
o	X	o	O	u	A	O	b

Directions Have children identify and write uppercase *O* and lowercase *o*. Then have them circle all the *O*'s and *o*'s in the box.

Remind children to write the upper- and lowercase letters so they can be easily read, using a left-to-right and top-to-bottom progression.

Letter Names

Kindergarten, Unit 1

Name _____

Nouns for People

1.

2.

3.

Directions Have children look at the first row of pictures and underline the mother. Have them look at the second row and underline the father. Then have them look at the third row and underline the grandmother. Then have children identify the pictures of the grown-ups in each row and draw a circle around them. Tell children to draw a picture in the box of someone in their family. Have them label their picture and then tell about it.

Grammar

Kindergarten, Unit 1

Name _____

Aa Bb Cc Dd Ee Ff Gg Hh Ii Jj Kk Ll Mm

Nn Oo Pp Qq Rr Ss Tt Uu Vv Ww Xx Yy Zz

P p P p

B	m	P	p	H	q	U	a
g	P	p	R	p	J	c	P
D	o	A	p	P	x	P	p
p	Y	p	P	v	P	P	p

Directions Have children identify and write uppercase *P* and lowercase *p*. Then have them circle all the *P*'s and *p*'s in the box.

Remind children to write the upper- and lowercase letters so they can be easily read, using a left-to-right and top-to-bottom progression.

9

like

1. I _____

2. I _____

3. I _____

4. I _____

Directions Have children read the word *I* and name each picture. Then have them write the word *like* to complete each sentence. Have children read the completed sentences aloud.

Have children point to and say the names of letters they recognize on the page. Then have children tap their desks once for each word as they read the sentences aloud again. Have children say other sentences with the word *like*.

Words to Know

Kindergarten, Unit 1

Name _____

Aa Bb Cc Dd Ee Ff Gg Hh Ii Jj Kk Ll Mm

Nn Oo Pp Qq Rr Ss Tt Uu Vv Ww Xx Yy Zz

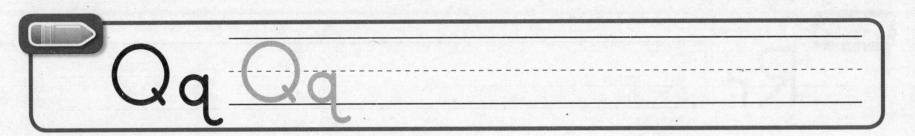

Qq *Qq*

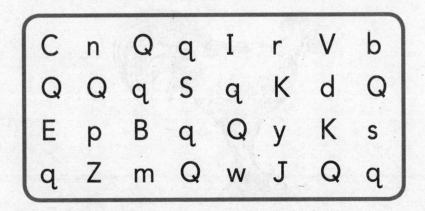

C	n	Q	q	I	r	V	b
Q	Q	q	S	q	K	d	Q
E	p	B	q	Q	y	K	s
q	Z	m	Q	w	J	Q	q

Directions Have children identify and write uppercase *Q* and lowercase *q*. Then have them circle all the *Q*'s and *q*'s in the box.

Remind children to write the upper- and lowercase letters so they can be easily read, using a left-to-right and top-to-bottom progression.

Name _____

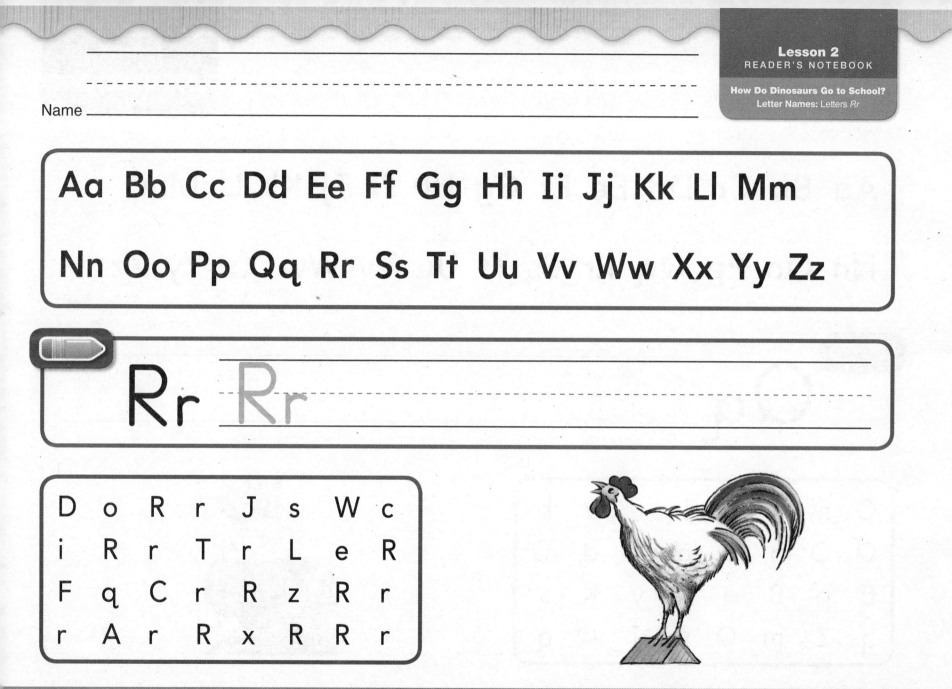

Aa Bb Cc Dd Ee Ff Gg Hh Ii Jj Kk Ll Mm

Nn Oo Pp Qq Rr Ss Tt Uu Vv Ww Xx Yy Zz

R r   R r

D	o	R	r	J	s	W	c
i	R	r	T	r	L	e	R
F	q	C	r	R	z	R	r
r	A	r	R	x	R	R	r

Directions Have children identify and write uppercase *R* and lowercase *r*. Then have them circle all the *R*'s and *r*'s in the box.

Remind children to write the upper- and lowercase letters so they can be easily read, using a left-to-right and top-to-bottom progression.

Name _____

Understanding Characters

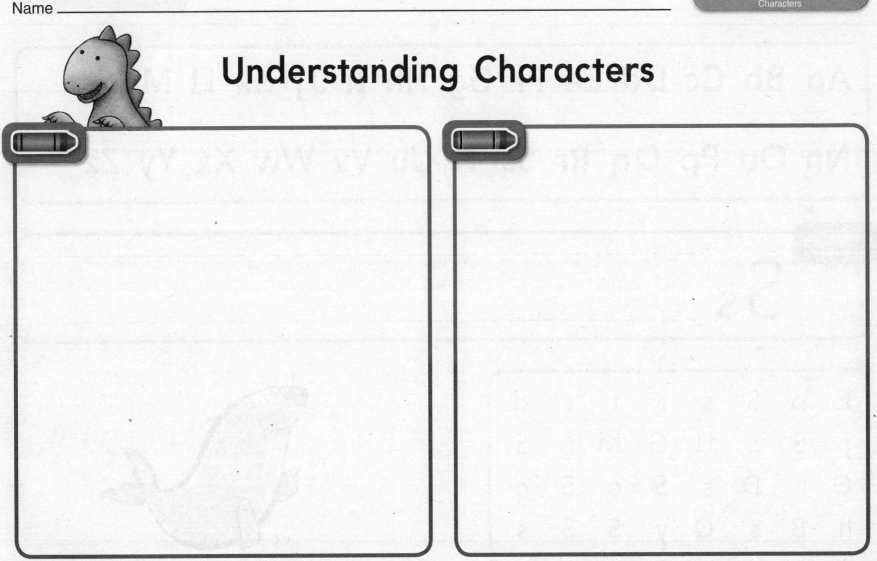

Directions Tell children to draw a picture that shows how their favorite character feels in the story. Then have them draw a picture to show how they would feel if they were in a classroom with a dinosaur. Have children share their pictures and talk about both. Tell them to speak clearly and use complete sentences as they share their ideas about the characters with classmates.

Kindergarten, Unit 1

Name _____

Aa Bb Cc Dd Ee Ff Gg Hh Ii Jj Kk Ll Mm

Nn Oo Pp Qq Rr Ss Tt Uu Vv Ww Xx Yy Zz

S s S s _____

E	p	S	s	K	t	s	d
j	S	s	U	G	M	f	S
G	r	D	s	S	a	S	o
h	B	s	Q	y	S	S	s

Directions Have children identify and write uppercase *S* and lowercase *s*. Then have them circle all the *S*'s and *s*'s in the box.

Remind children to write the upper- and lowercase letters so they can be easily read, using a left-to-right and top-to-bottom progression.

Name _____

Aa Bb Cc Dd Ee Ff Gg Hh Ii Jj Kk Ll Mm

Nn Oo Pp Qq Rr Ss Tt Uu Vv Ww Xx Yy Zz

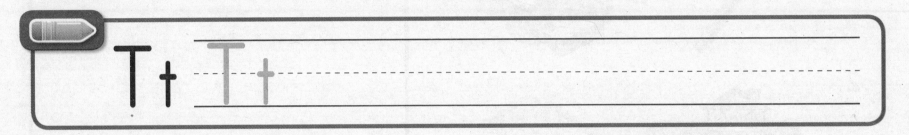

T t

F	q	T	t	L	u	Y	e
j	T	t	V	t	N	g	T
H	s	E	t	T	b	T	t
t	C	t	T	z	T	T	t

Directions Have children identify and write uppercase *T* and lowercase *t*. Then have them circle all the *T*'s and *t*'s in the box.

Remind children to write the upper- and lowercase letters so they can be easily read, using a left-to-right and top-to-bottom progression.

Letter Names

15

Kindergarten, Unit 1

Nouns for Places

Directions Have children name the pictures in the first row. Have them underline the picture that shows a place. Repeat for the second and third rows.

Then have children draw a picture of a favorite place in the box. Have them label their picture and then tell about it.

Name _____

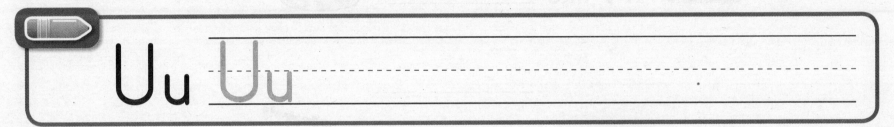

Aa Bb Cc Dd Ee Ff Gg Hh Ii Jj Kk Ll Mm

Nn Oo Pp Qq Rr Ss Tt Uu Vv Ww Xx Yy Zz

Uu Uu

G	r	U	r	M	v	Z	f
k	U	u	W	p	O	h	U
I	t	F	u	U	c	U	d
A	D	u	B	a	U	Y	u

Directions Have children identify and write uppercase *U* and lowercase *u*. Then have them circle all the *U*'s and *u*'s in the box.

Remind children to write the upper- and lowercase letters so they can be easily read, using a left-to-right and top-to-bottom progression.

Letter Names

Kindergarten, Unit 1

Name _____

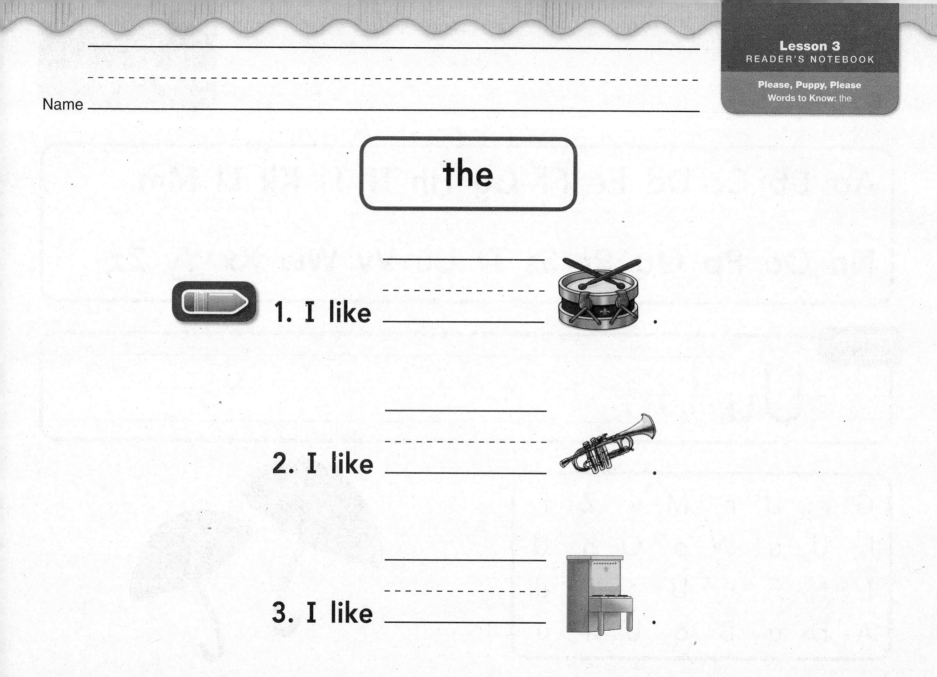

the

1. I like _____

2. I like _____

3. I like _____

Directions Have children read the words *I like* and name each picture. Then have them write the word *the* to complete each sentence. Have children read the completed sentences aloud.

Have children point to and say the names of letters they recognize on the page. Then have children tap their desks once for each word as they read the sentences aloud again. Have children say other sentences with the word *the*.

Name _____

Aa Bb Cc Dd Ee Ff Gg Hh Ii Jj Kk Ll Mm

Nn Oo Pp Qq Rr Ss Tt Uu Vv Ww Xx Yy Zz

Vv Vv

H	s	V	v	N	w	A	f
l	V	v	X	v	P	i	V
J	u	G	v	V	d	V	v
v	E	v	V	b	V	V	v

Directions Have children identify and write uppercase *V* and lowercase *v*. Then have them circle all the *V*'s and *v*'s in the box.

Remind children to write the upper- and lowercase letters so they can be easily read, using a left-to-right and top-to-bottom progression.

Name _____

Aa Bb Cc Dd Ee Ff Gg Hh Ii Jj Kk Ll Mm

Nn Oo Pp Qq Rr Ss Tt Uu Vv Ww Xx Yy Zz

Ww Ww

I	t	T	w	O	x	B	g
m	J	w	Y	w	Q	j	W
W	v	H	w	W	e	W	q
w	F	w	Y	c	W	X	w

Directions Have children identify and write uppercase *W* and lowercase *w*. Then have them circle all the *W*'s and *w*'s in the box.

Remind children to write the upper- and lowercase letters so they can be easily read, using a left-to-right and top-to-bottom progression.

Name _____

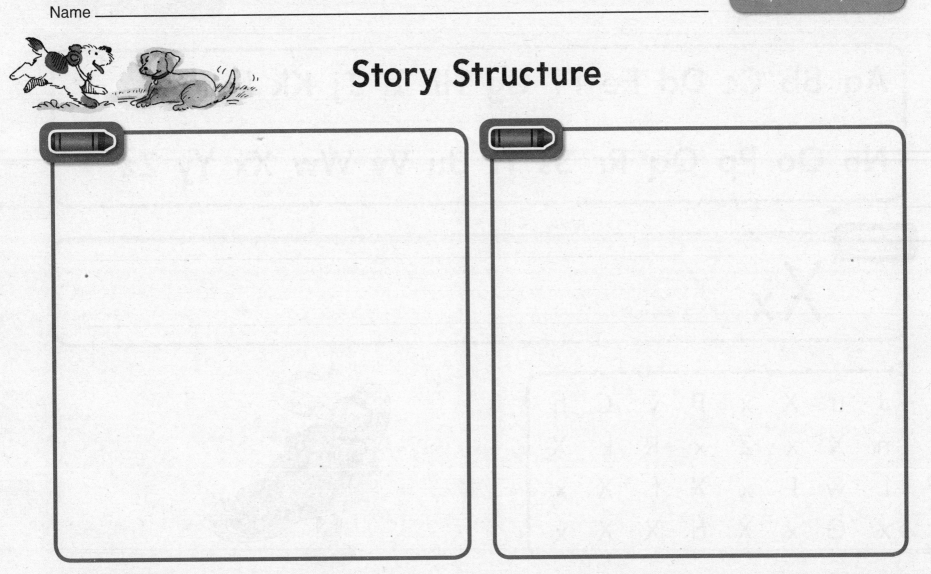

Story Structure

Directions Tell children to draw a picture of the main character in the story. Have them also show the setting in the background. Then have them draw a picture to show their favorite event in the story. Have children share their pictures and describe their drawings. Then have them retell or act out the key event they illustrated.

Comprehension
© Houghton Mifflin Harcourt Publishing Company. All rights reserved.

Kindergarten, Unit 1

Name _____

Aa Bb Cc Dd Ee Ff Gg Hh Ii Jj Kk Ll Mm

Nn Oo Pp Qq Rr Ss Tt Uu Vv Ww Xx Yy Zz

Xx Xx

J	u	X	x	P	y	C	h
n	X	x	Z	x	R	k	X
L	w	I	x	X	f	X	x
x	G	x	X	d	X	X	x

Directions Have children identify and write uppercase *X* and lowercase *x*. Then have them circle all the *X*'s and *x*'s in the box.

Remind children to write the upper- and lowercase letters so they can be easily read, using a left-to-right and top-to-bottom progression.

22

Name _____

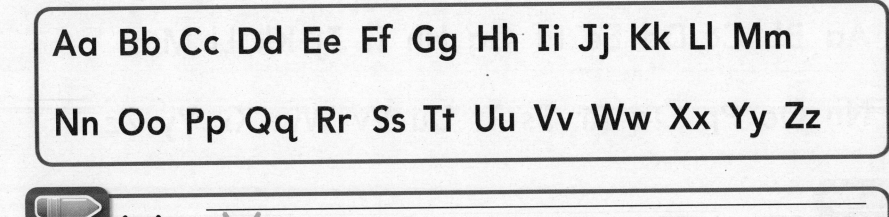

Aa Bb Cc Dd Ee Ff Gg Hh Ii Jj Kk Ll Mm

Nn Oo Pp Qq Rr Ss Tt Uu Vv Ww Xx Yy Zz

Yy _____

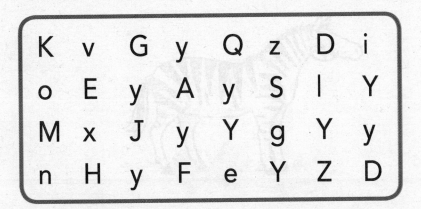

K	v	G	y	Q	z	D	i
o	E	y	A	y	S	l	Y
M	x	J	y	Y	g	Y	y
n	H	y	F	e	Y	Z	D

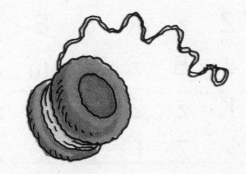

Directions Have children identify and write uppercase *Y* and lowercase *y*. Then have them circle all the *Y*'s and *y*'s in the box.

Remind children to write the upper- and lowercase letters so they can be easily read, using a left-to-right and top-to-bottom progression.

Letter Names

Kindergarten, Unit 1

Name _____

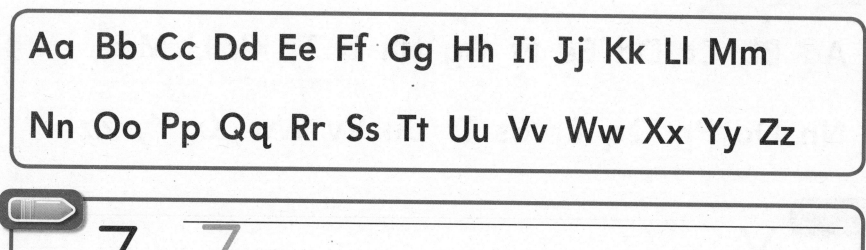

Aa Bb Cc Dd Ee Ff Gg Hh Ii Jj Kk Ll Mm

Nn Oo Pp Qq Rr Ss Tt Uu Vv Ww Xx Yy Zz

Zz Zz

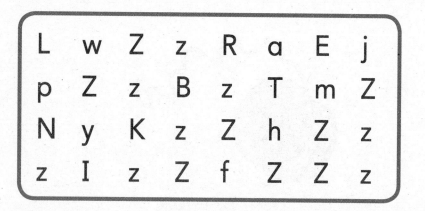

L	w	Z	z	R	a	E	j
p	Z	z	B	z	T	m	Z
N	y	K	z	Z	h	Z	z
z	I	z	Z	f	Z	Z	z

Directions Have children identify and write uppercase *Z* and lowercase *z*. Then have them circle all the *Z*'s and *z*'s in the box.

Remind children to write the upper- and lowercase letters so they can be easily read, using a left-to-right and top-to-bottom progression.

Name

Nouns for Animals and Things

1.

2.

3.

Directions Have children name the pictures in the first row. Have them tell whether each picture shows an animal or a thing. Have them underline the picture that shows an animal and draw a circle around the picture that shows a thing.

Repeat for the second and third rows. Then have children draw a picture in the box of a favorite animal or thing. Have them dictate or write a caption for their picture.

Grammar

Kindergarten, Unit 1

Name _____

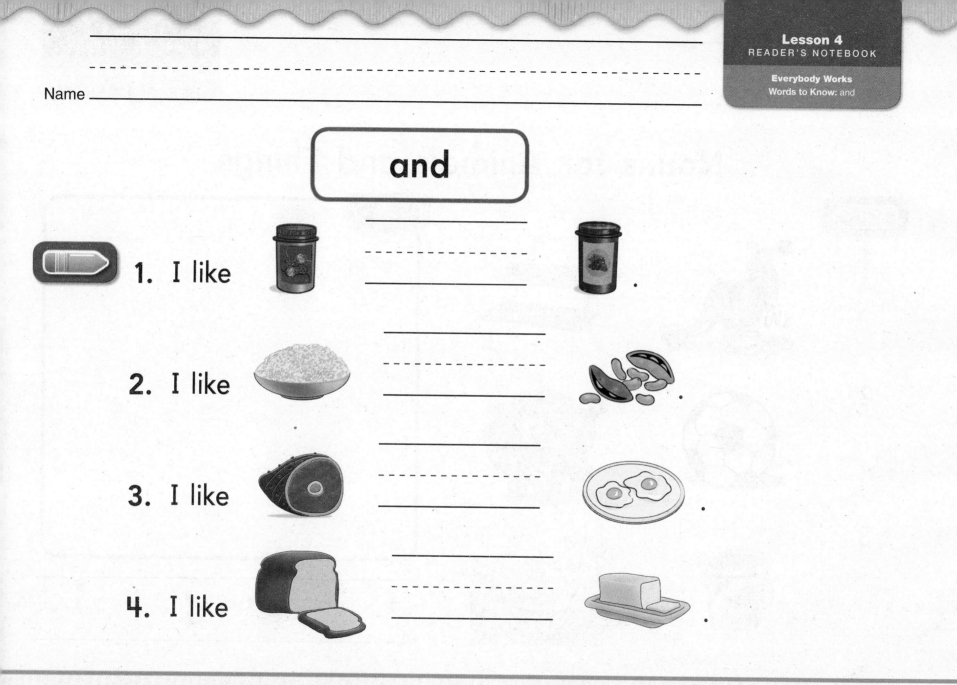

and

1. I like _____ .

2. I like _____

3. I like _____ .

4. I like _____ .

Directions Have children read the words *I like* and name each picture. Then have them write the word *and* to complete each sentence. Have children read the completed sentences aloud.

Have children point to and say the names of letters they recognize on the page. Then have children tap their desks once for each word as they read the sentences aloud again. Have children say other sentences with the word *and*.

Name _____

1. m Mm M m

2.

Directions Have children name the Alphafriend and its letter. Have them trace and write *M* and *m*. Then name the pictures (*monkey, mittens, truck, man, motorcycle, mug, milk, moose*) and have children write *Mm* next to the pictures whose names start with the /m/ sound. Help children think of groups of words that begin with the /m/ sound. For example, *My monkey moves more*.

Phonics

Kindergarten, Unit 1

Name _____

1.  **m** **Mm**   Mm

2.

Phonics

28

Kindergarten, Unit 1

Name _____

Text and Graphic Features

1.

2.

Directions Tell children to look at the first set of pictures. Have them circle the picture that best shows a man who helps children cross the street. Have children identify the sign and explain why the man is holding it. Then have them look at the second set of pictures and circle the picture that best shows a girl who delivers newspapers. Discuss with children how they matched your spoken words to the correct picture. Then ask children how pictures can help them better understand information in a text.

Comprehension

29

Kindergarten, Unit 1

Action Verbs in the Present Tense

I like

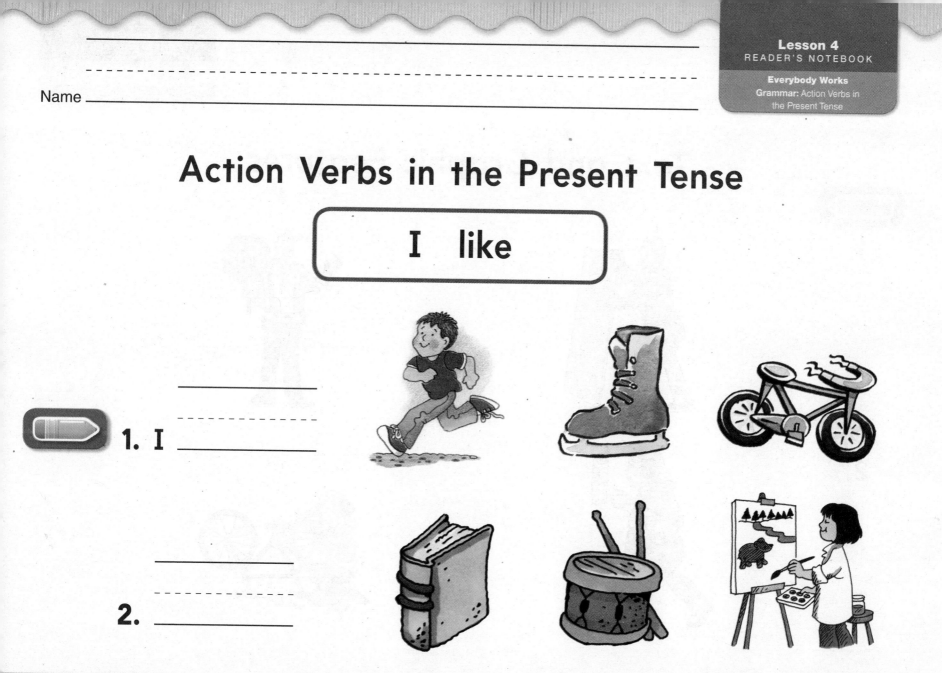

1. I _____

2. _____

Name _____

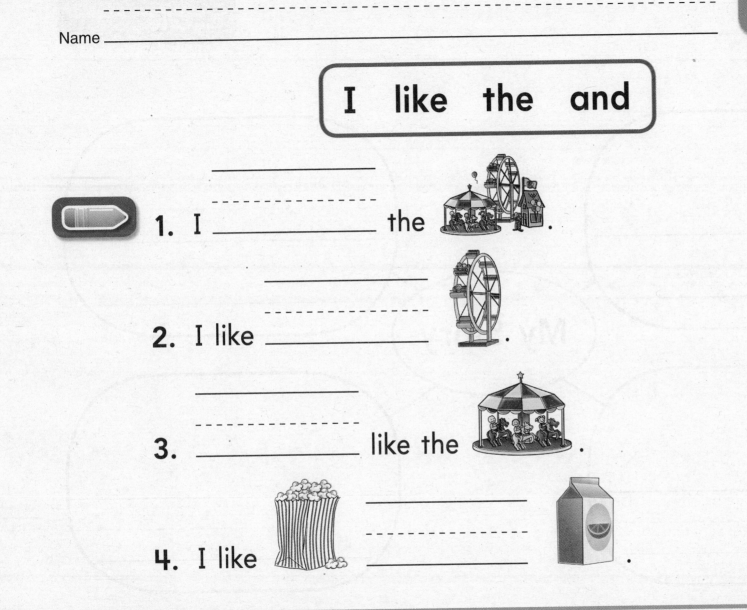

I   like   the   and

1. I _____ the 🎡 .

2. I like _____ .

3. _____ like the 🎠 .

4. I like _____ .

Have children point to and say the names of the letters they recognize on the page. Then have them read the sentences aloud again and tap their desks once for each word. Have children tell a story using all of the Words to Know.

Kindergarten, Unit 1

Name _____

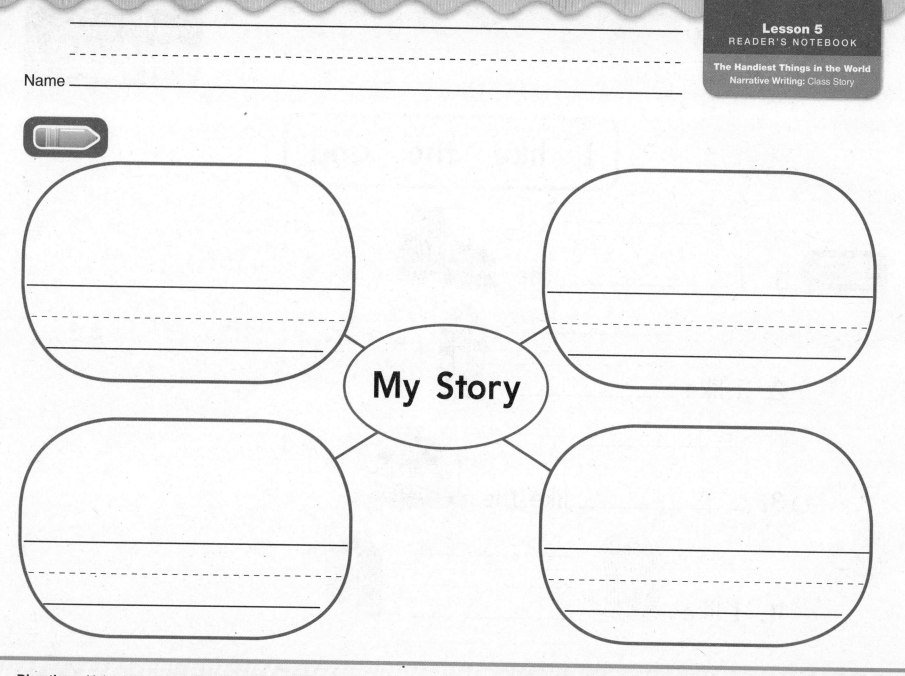

My Story

Directions Help children **generate ideas** for their own story. Have children write ideas and draw pictures in the space provided in the idea web. Guide children to write words or draw pictures showing the characters, setting, and what will happen in their stories.

Kindergarten, Unit 1

Name _____

1. S S s ‑ ‑ S s ‑ ‑ ‑ ‑ ‑ ‑ ‑ ‑ ‑ ‑ ‑ ‑

2.

Directions Have children name the Alphafriend and its letter. Have them trace and write *Ss*. Then have them write *Ss* next to the pictures whose names start with the /s/ sound.

Help children think of groups of words that begin with the /s/ sound. For example, *Sarah says six sentences.*

Name _____

My Story

Directions Have children use pages 34–35 to draft, revise, and edit a story. Encourage children to use their ideas from **Reader's Notebook** page 32 as a guide in their writing. As children **develop their drafts,** remind them that they will have a chance to add to their story on another day. Remind children to include events for the beginning, middle, and end of their story. As children **revise their drafts,** discuss sentences and details they could add to make their story even better. Remind children to include a sentence at the end that tells about their reaction to the story. As children **edit their drafts,** help them use what they know about letters and sounds to check the spelling of words. Have them check spelling using other sources as appropriate. Have children also check their sentences for correct capitalization and punctuation.

Name _____

My Story

_____
- - - - - - - - - - - - - - - - - - - -
_____
_____
- - - - - - - - - - - - - - - - - - - -
_____
_____
- - - - - - - - - - - - - - - - - - - -
_____

Directions Have children use pages 34–35 to draft, revise, and edit a story. Encourage children to use their ideas from **Reader's Notebook** page 32 as a guide in their writing. As children **develop their drafts,** remind them that they will have a chance to add to their story on another day. Remind children to include events for the beginning, middle, and end of their story. As children **revise their drafts,** discuss sentences and details they could add to make their story even better. Remind children to include a sentence at the end that tells about their reaction to the story. As children **edit their drafts,** help them use what they know about letters and sounds to check the spelling of words. Have them check spelling using other sources as appropriate. Have children also check their sentences for correct capitalization and punctuation.

Name

1. Mm Mm   Ss Ss

2.

Directions Have children name each letter. Have them write *Mm* and *Ss*. Then tell children to name the pictures and write the letter for the sound they hear at the beginning of each picture name.

Remind children to write the upper- and lowercase letters so they can be easily read, using a left-to-right and top-to-bottom progression.

Name _____

Details

Directions Have children draw one of the handy tools from the **Big Book.** Have them share their pictures with a group. Have children explain how the tool makes a job or activity easier.

Remind them to speak clearly and use complete sentences as they describe the tools and how they help people do things.

37

Kindergarten, Unit 1

Name _____

Action Verbs in the Present Tense

I   like

1. I _____

2. _____ like

Directions Have children name each picture. Have them complete each sentence by writing a word from the box and circling the picture that shows an action.

Have children read their sentences aloud using an action word to describe the picture they circled. Tell them to speak clearly as they share their sentences and to listen carefully to others as they share.

Name _____

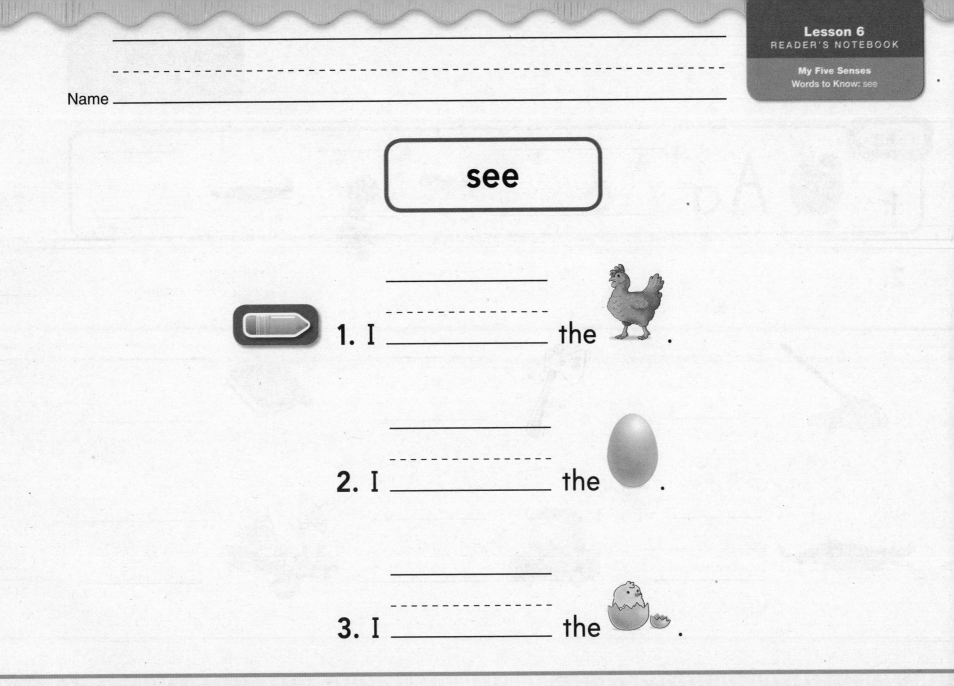

see

1. I _____ the 🐔 .

2. I _____ the 🥚 .

3. I _____ the 🐣 .

Directions Have children read the word in the box and name each picture. Then have them write the word *see* to complete each sentence. Have children read the completed sentences aloud.

Have children point to and say the names of letters they recognize on the page. Then have children tap their desks once for each word as they read the sentences aloud again. Have children say other sentences with the word *see*.

Words to Know

39

Kindergarten, Unit 2

Name _____

1.

2.

Directions Have children write their name at the top of the page. Have them name the **Alphafriend** and its letter, and trace and write *A* and *a*. Then help children name the pictures (*ant, alligator, mop, ax, book, alligator, car, astronaut*) and have them write *Aa* next to the ones whose names start with the /ă/ sound. Help children think of groups of words that begin with short *a*, the /ă/ sound. Example: *attic, actor, apple*.

Name _____

1. Aa _____ Aa _____ Mm _____ Mm

2.

Directions Have children write their name at the top of the page. Have them trace and write *Aa* and *Mm*. Then help children name the pictures (*monkey, ax, alligator, motorbike, mittens,* *ambulance*) and write the capital and lowercase letters that stand for the sound they hear at the beginning of each name.

Remind children to write the upper- and lowercase letters so they can be easily read, using a left-to-right and top-to-bottom progression.

Phonics

41

Kindergarten, Unit 2

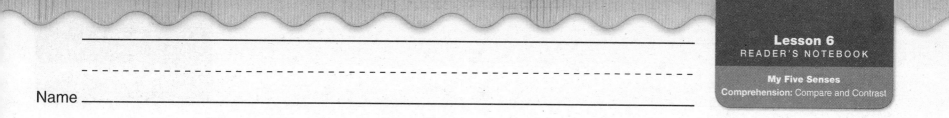
Name _____

Compare and Contrast

 1. I can taste the  .

3.

2. I can touch the 🐰 .

Name _____

Sensory Words

Directions Tell children to look at and name the pictures. Have children draw a line from each sense in the top row to the picture it describes in the bottom row. Have children write a complete sentence that describes one of the pictures. Have them include sensory words in their sentences. Have them share their sentences with the class.

Name _____

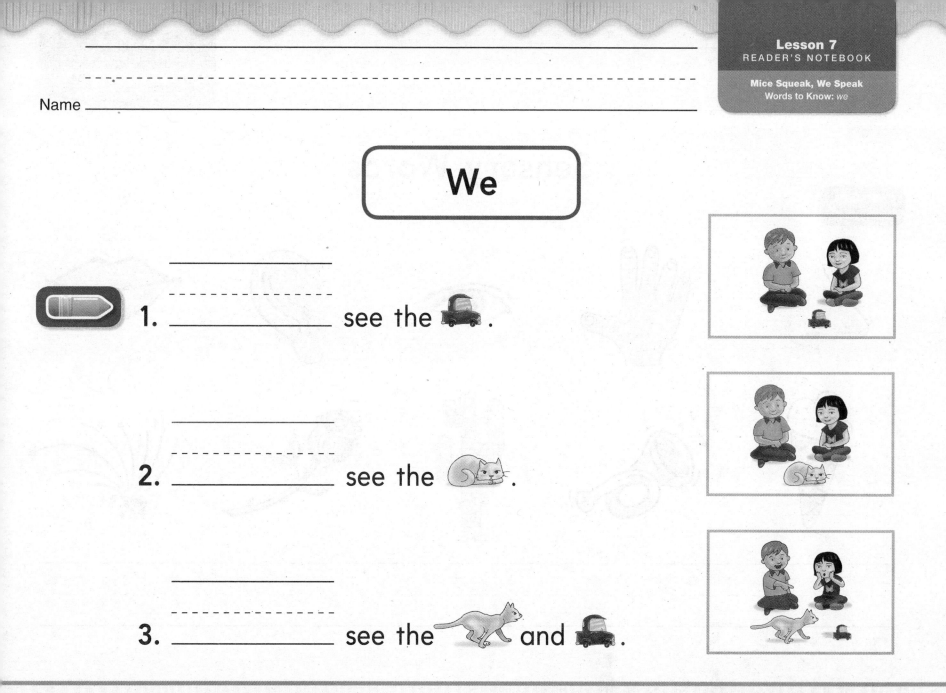

We

1. _____ see the 🚗 .

2. _____ see the 🐱 .

3. _____ see the 🐱 and 🚗 .

Directions Have children write their name at the top of the page. Have children read the word in the box and name each picture. Then have them write the word *We* to complete each sentence. Have children read the completed sentences aloud.

Have children point to and say the names of letters they recognize on the page. Then have children tap their desks once for each word as they read the sentences aloud again. Have children say other sentences with the word *we*.

Name _____

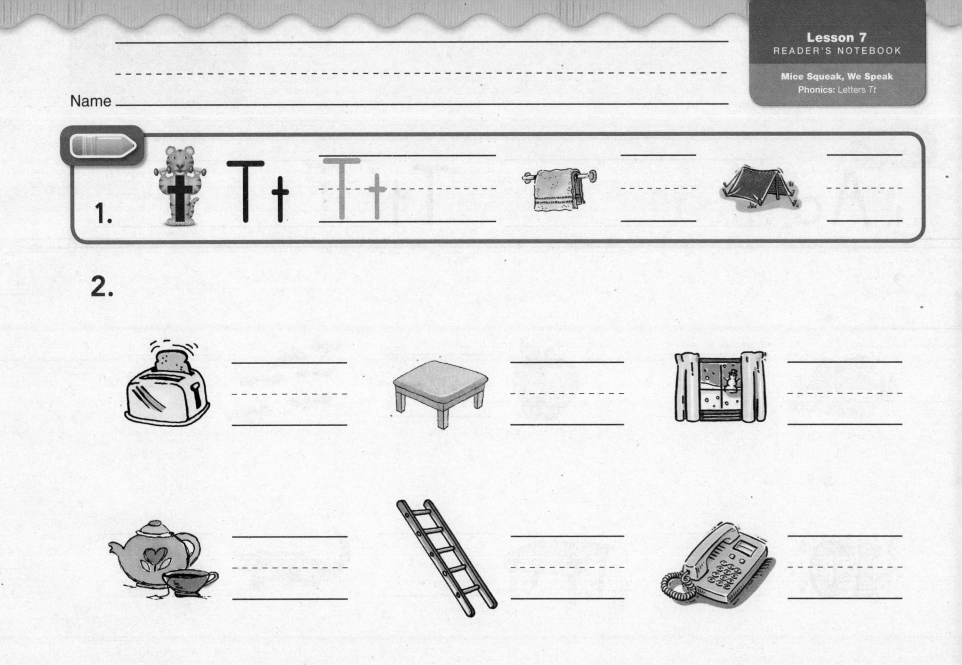

1.

2.

Directions Have children write their name at the top of the page. Have children trace and write *T* and *t*. Then help them name the pictures (*towel, tent, toaster, table, window, tea,* *ladder, telephone*). Have children write *Tt* next to the pictures whose names start with the /t/ sound.

Help children think of groups of words that begin with the /t/ sound. For example, *tiger, touchdown, trumpet, taste.*

Name _____

1. Aa Aa   Tt Tt

2.

Remind children to write the upper- and lowercase letters so they can be easily read, using a left-to-right and top-to-bottom progression.

Name _____

Understanding Characters

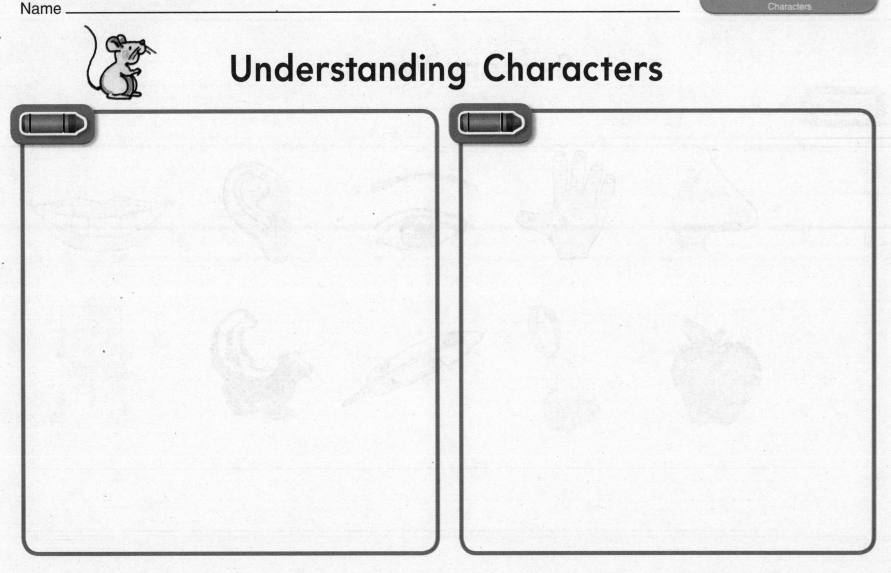

Directions Tell children to draw a picture of their favorite animal character from *Mice Squeak, We Speak*. Then have them draw a picture to show how they think the animal feels when it makes its sound.

Have children share their pictures. Page through the Big Book and have children identify each character.

Name _____

Sensory Words

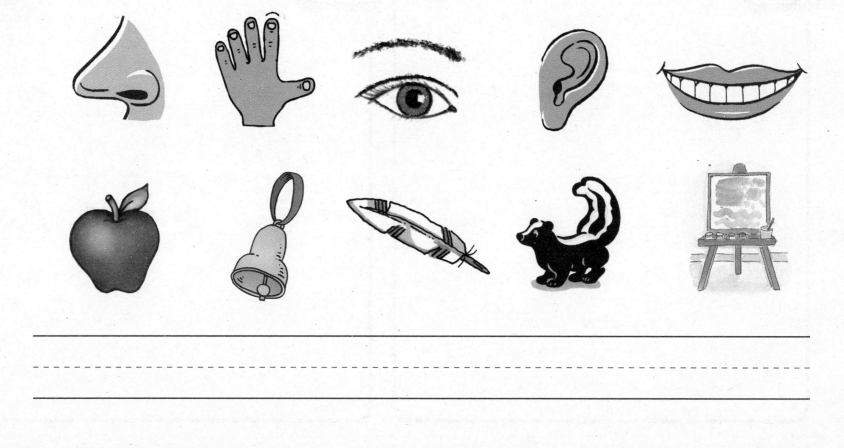

Directions Have children name the pictures in each row. Have them draw a line from each sense in the top row to the picture it describes in the bottom row. Then have children write a complete sentence that describes one of the pictures.

Have them include sensory words in their sentences. Ask children to share their sentences with the class.

Grammar
Kindergarten, Unit 2

Name _____

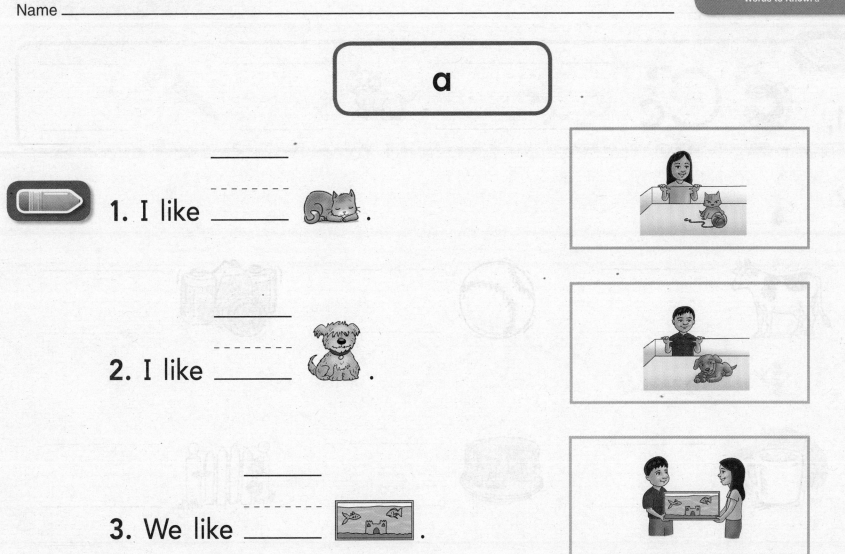

a

1. I like _____ 🐱 .

2. I like _____ 🐕 .

3. We like _____ 🐠 .

Directions Have children write their name at the top of the page. Then have them read the word in the box, name each rebus picture (*cat, dog, fish tank*), and write the word *a* to complete each sentence. Have children read the completed sentences aloud.

Have children point to and say the names of letters they recognize on the page. Then have them tap their desks once for each word as they read the sentences aloud again. Have children say other sentences with the word *a*.

49

Name _____

1. C Cc Cc _____ _____

2.

_____

_____

_____

_____

_____

_____

Directions Have children write their name at the top of the page. Have them name the Alphafriend and its letter and trace and write *C* and *c*. Then name the pictures together (cat, carrot, cow, ball, camera, cup, cake, gate) and have children write *Cc* next to the pictures whose names start with the /k/ sound. Help children think of groups of words that begin with the /k/ sound, for example, *cart, cupcake, cap*.

Name _____

1. Aa Aa _____ Cc Cc _____

2.

Directions Have children write their name at the top of the page. Then have them name and write *Aa* and *Cc*. Name the pictures together (alligator, candle, cup, axe, ants, camera) and ask children to write the capital and lowercase letters for the sound they hear at the beginning of each picture name.

Remind children to write the upper- and lowercase letters so they can be easily read, using a left-to-right and top-to-bottom progression.

Phonics

51

Kindergarten, Unit 2

Name _____

Details

Directions Tell children to draw a picture of one of the animals in the Big Book. Have them share their pictures with the class. Have children use describing words to tell what the animal looks like and how it moves.

Remind them to speak clearly and use complete sentences as they describe their pictures. Then have children tell which words are describing words.

Kindergarten, Unit 2

Adjectives for Color

purple   red   brown

1. Look at the _____ wagon.

2. I have a pair of _____ mittens.

3. It is a _____ coat.

4. _____

Directions Discuss the pictures with children and read each sentence frame aloud. Have children complete each sentence frame by writing a color word from the box on the line.

Then have children write a complete sentence using a color word to describe something. Have them share their sentences with the class.

Name _____

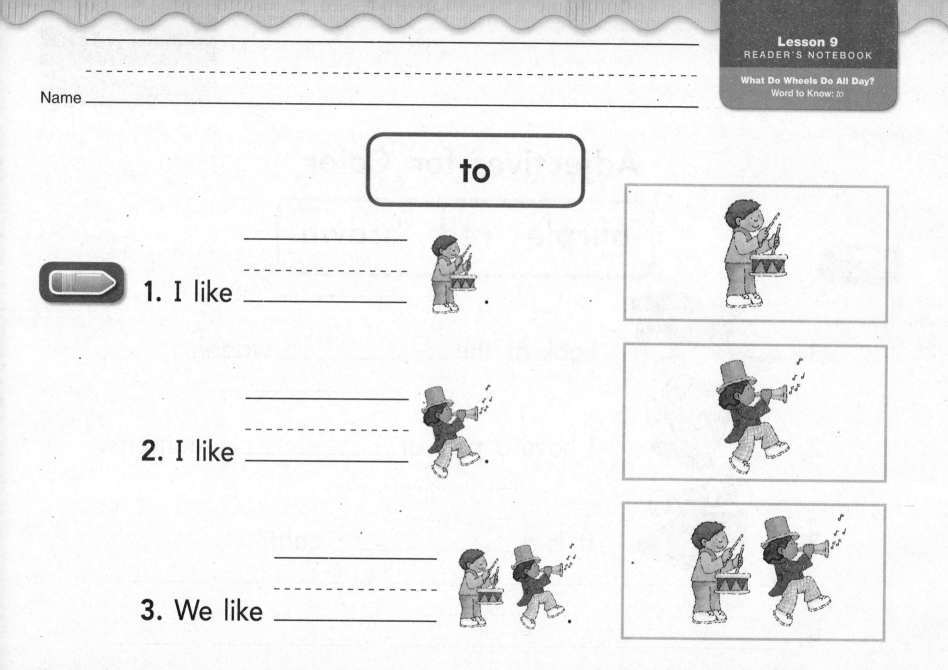

to

1. I like _____ .

2. I like _____ .

3. We like _____ .

Have children read the word in the box and name each picture. Then have them write the word *to* to complete each sentence. Have children read the completed sentences aloud.

Have children point to and say the names of letters they recognize on the page. Then have children tap their desks once for each word as they read the sentences aloud again. Have children say other sentences with the word *to*.

Name _____

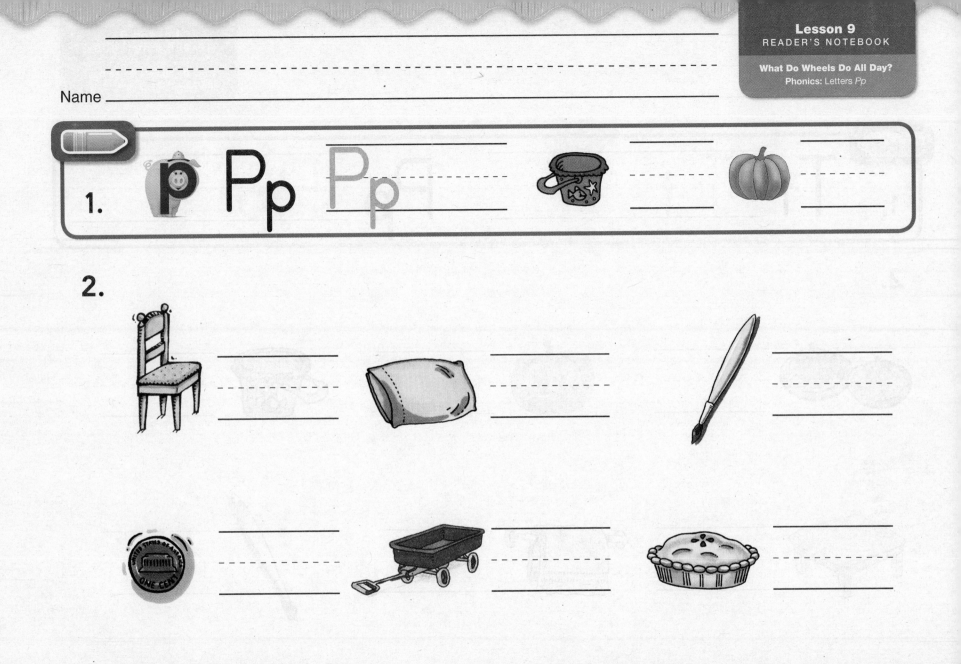

1.

2.

Directions Have children name the Alphafriend and its letter. Have them trace and write *P* and *p*. Then name the pictures together (*pail, pumpkin, chair, pillow, paintbrush, penny, wagon, pie*).

Have children write *Pp* next to the pictures whose names start with the /p/ sound.

Help children think of groups of words that begin with the /p/ sound, for example, *puppy, pillow, package*.

Phonics

Kindergarten, Unit 2

Name _____

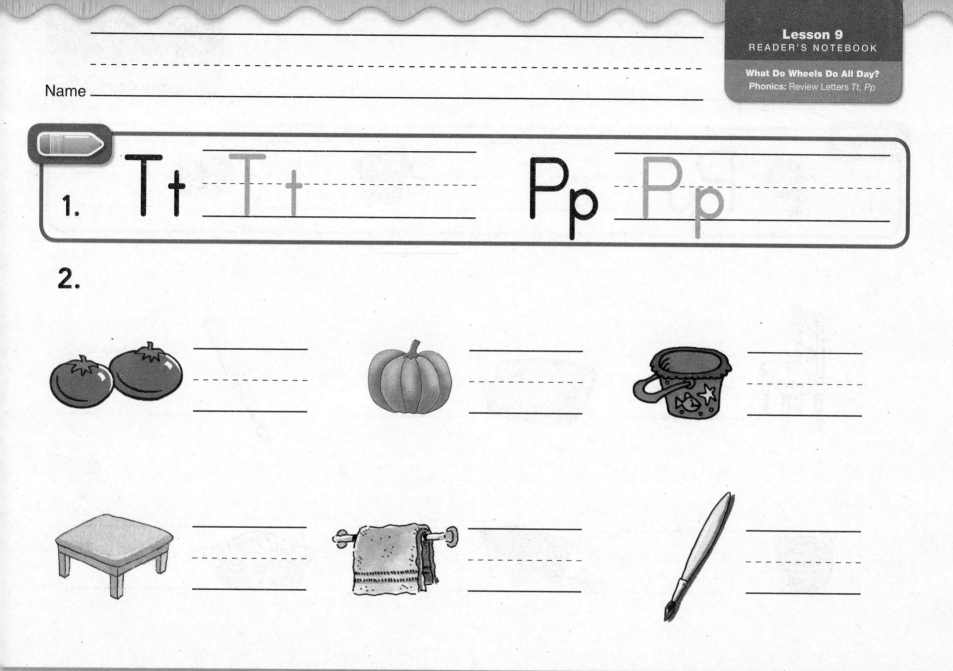

1. T t T t   P p P p

2.

Directions Have children name each letter. Have them trace and write *Tt* and *Pp*. Then help children name the pictures (*tomatoes, pumpkin, pail, table, towel, paintbrush*). Have children write the capital and lowercase letters for the sound they hear at the beginning of each name.

Remind children to write the upper- and lowercase letters so they can be easily read, using a left-to-right and top-to-bottom progression.

Name _____

Text and Graphic Features

1.

2.

Directions Tell children to look at the first row of pictures. Have them circle the picture that best shows wheels helping people to win a race. Then have them look at the second row of pictures and circle the picture that best shows wheels helping people get from place to place. Discuss with children how pictures can help them better understand information they read about. Then have children use action words, such as *roll, whiz, spin,* to describe how wheels move. Have them name the action words.

57

Comprehension

Name _____

Adjectives for Numbers

| seven   two   five |

1. The bike has _____ wheels.

2. The _____ ducks swim.

3. There are _____ hats.

4. _____

Directions Discuss the pictures with children and read each sentence frame aloud. Have children complete each sentence frame by writing a word from the box on the line.

Then have children write a complete sentence using one of the number words. Have them share their sentences with the class.

Grammar

58

Name _____

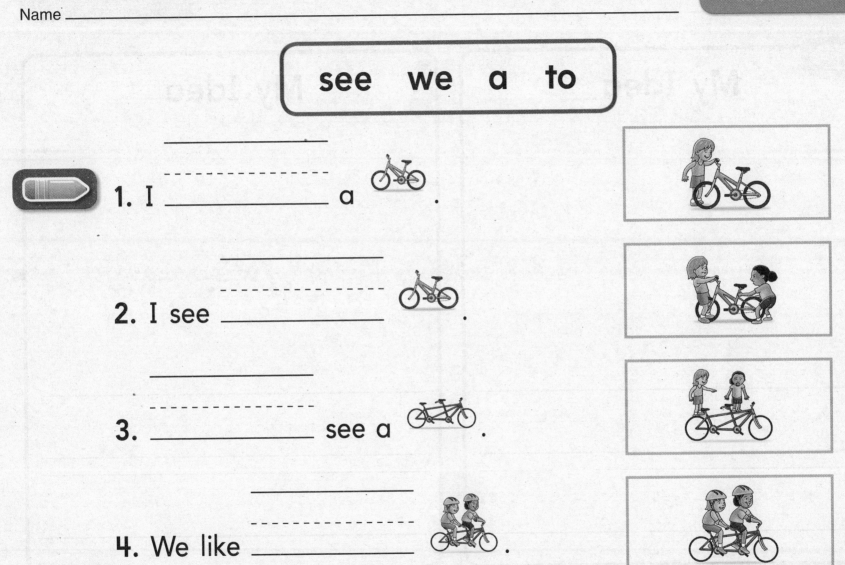

see   we   a   to

1. I _____ a 🚲 .

2. I see _____ .

3. _____ see a 🚲 .

4. We like _____ 🚲 .

Directions Remind children to write their names. Have children read the words in the box and name each picture. Then have them write the word *see, we, a,* or *to* to complete each sentence. Guide children to capitalize *we* at the beginning of the third sentence. Have children read the completed sentences aloud. Then have children tell a story about the page, using all of the Words to Know.

Words to Know

Kindergarten, Unit 2

Name _____

My Idea

My Idea

Directions Help children **generate ideas** for their own informative descriptions.

Guide children to draw pictures of the things they are thinking of writing about. Then have children write words that describe each idea. Remind them to include details about size and shape.

Name _____

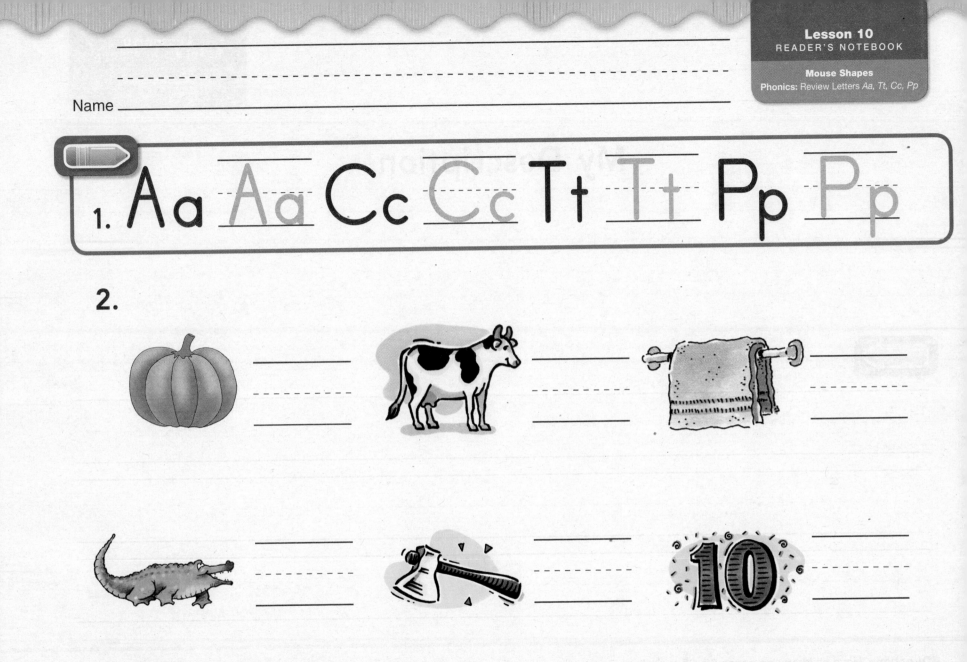

1. Aa Aa Cc Cc Tt Tt Pp Pp

2.

Name _____

My Description

Directions Have children use pages 62–63 to draft, revise, and edit an informative description. Encourage children to use their ideas from **Reader's Notebook** page 60 as a guide in their writing. As children **develop their drafts**, remind them that they will have a chance to add to their description on another day. As children **revise their drafts**, discuss sentences and details they could add to make their description even better. For example, could they add some more shape and size adjectives? As children **edit their drafts**, help them use what they know about letters and sounds to check the spelling of words. Have them check spelling, using other sources as appropriate. Have children also check their sentences for correct capitalization and punctuation.

Name _____

My Description

_____

- -

_____

- -

_____

- -

Directions Have children use pages 62–63 to draft, revise, and edit an informative description. Encourage children to use their ideas from **Reader's Notebook** page 60 as a guide in their writing. As children **develop their drafts**, remind them that they will have a chance to add to their description on another day. As children **revise their drafts**, discuss sentences and details they could add to make their description even better. For example, could they add some more shape and size adjectives? As children **edit their drafts**, help them use what they know about letters and sounds to check the spelling of words. Have them check spelling, using other sources as appropriate. Have children also check their sentences for correct capitalization and punctuation.

Name _____

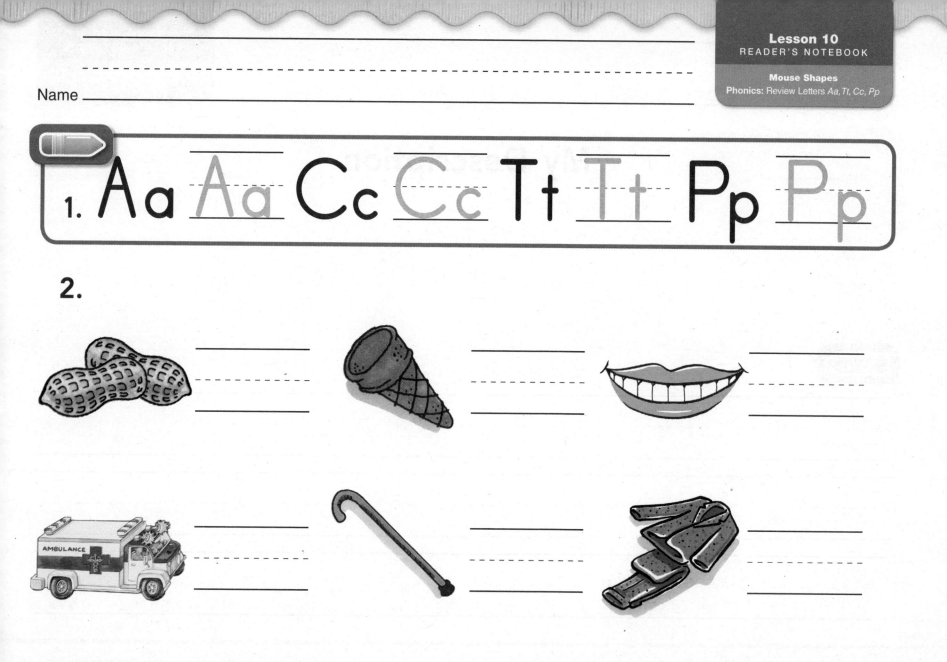

1. Aa Aa Cc Cc Tt Tt Pp Pp

2.

Directions Remind children to write their names. Then have children name each letter in row 1. Have them trace *Aa, Cc, Tt,* and *Pp*. Then help children name the pictures (*peanuts, cone, teeth, ambulance, cane, pajamas*) and write the capital and lowercase letters for the sound they hear at the beginning of each picture name. Remind children to write the upper- and lowercase letters so they can be easily read, using a left-to-right and top-to-bottom progression.

Phonics

Kindergarten, Unit 2

Name _____

Story Structure

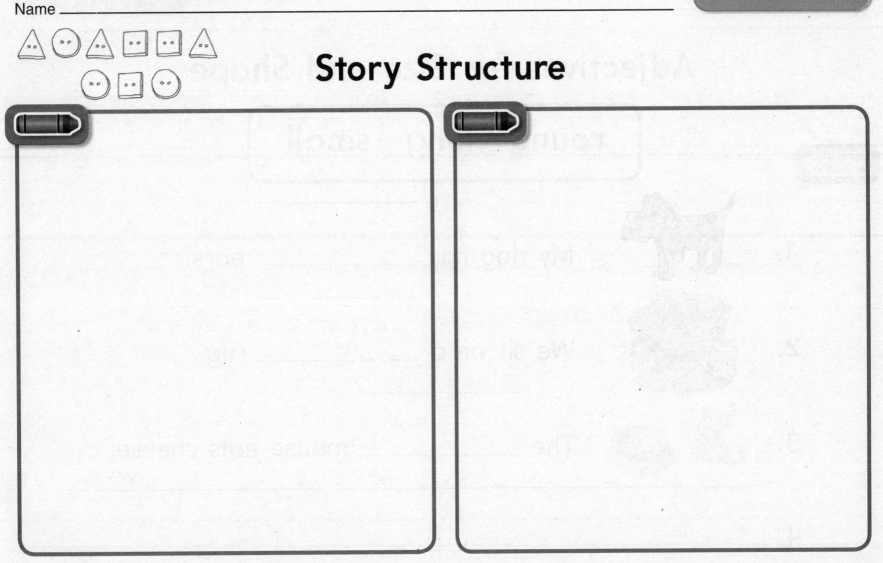

Directions Discuss with children who the Big Book story is about and where it takes place. Then have them draw a picture of something that happens at the beginning of the story and at the end of the story. Have children share their pictures.

Have them use location words, such as *above, below,* or *next to* to describe parts of their pictures. Then have children sort the shapes at the top of the page into categories. Have them color the circles red, the squares yellow, and the triangles blue.

Comprehension

Kindergarten, Unit 2

Name _____

Adjectives for Size and Shape

| round   long   small |

1. My dog has _____ ears.

2. We sit on a _____ rug.

3. The _____ mouse eats cheese.

4. _____

Directions Discuss the pictures with children and read each sentence frame aloud. Have children complete each sentence frame by writing a word from the box on the line. Have them circle the word that tells about shape and underline the words that tell about size. Then have children write a complete sentence using one of the size or shape words. Have them share their sentences with the class.

Grammar
© Houghton Mifflin Harcourt Publishing Company. All rights reserved.

Kindergarten, Unit 2

Name _____

come   me

1. I see Sam.

_____
2. Come to _____, Sam.

_____
3. _____ to me, Sam.

_____
4. See Sam _____!

Directions Have children read the words in the box and look at each picture. Then have them write the word *come* or *me* to complete each sentence. Guide children to capitalize *come* at the beginning of the third sentence. Then have children read the sentences aloud. Have children point to and say the names of letters they recognize on the page. Then have children identify the action verb. Have children say other sentences with the words *come* and *me*.

Words to Know

67

Kindergarten, Unit 3

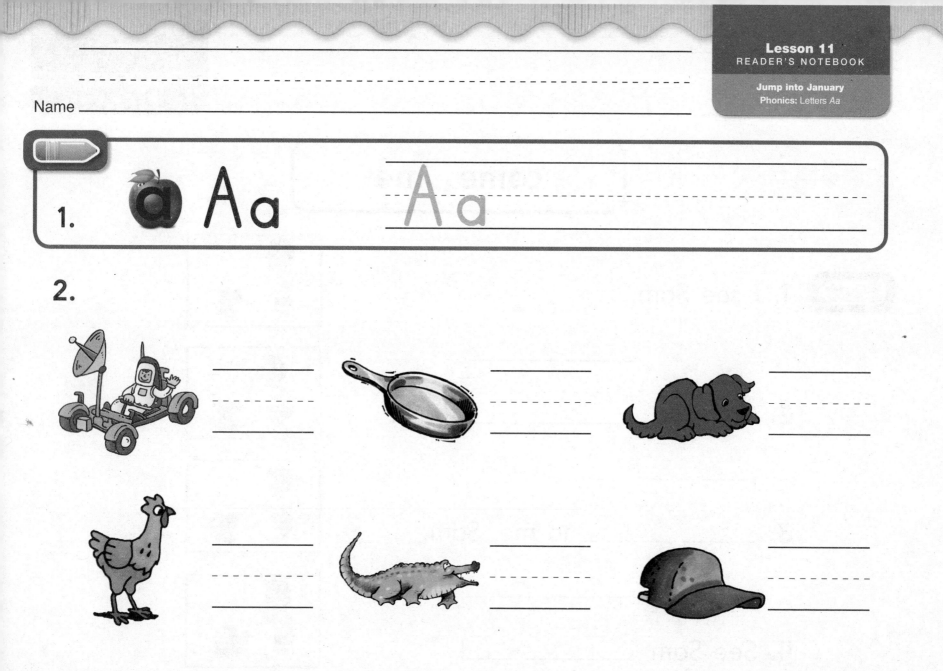

Name _____

1. 🍎a Aa   Aa

2.

Tell children to name each picture and write the letters Aa when they hear the short a sound somewhere in the word. Remind children to write the upper- and lowercase letters so they can be easily read, using a left-to-right and top-to-bottom progression.

Name _____

Words with *a*

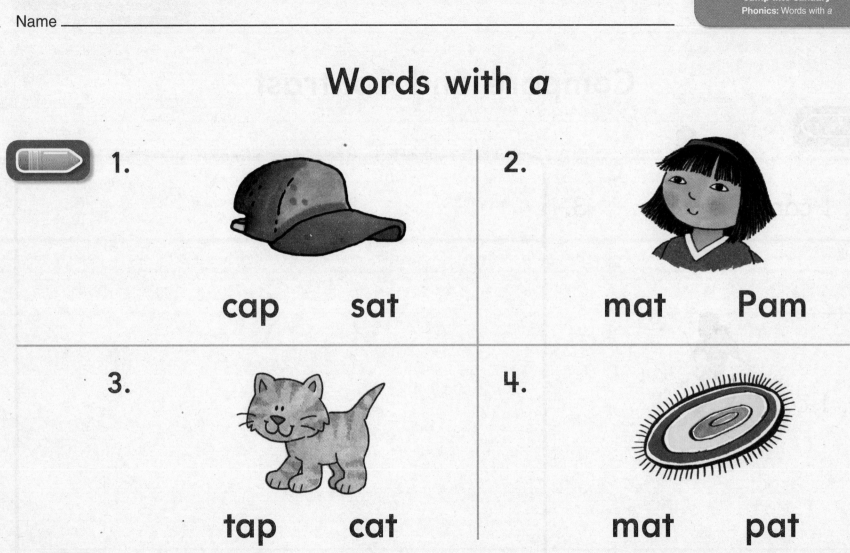

1. cap   sat

2. mat   Pam

3. tap   cat

4. mat   pat

Directions Tell children to look at the first picture. Then have them circle the word that matches the picture. Repeat with the rest of the pictures and words.

Have children say the words that match each picture. Then have them think of words that rhyme with each one.

Name _____

Compare and Contrast

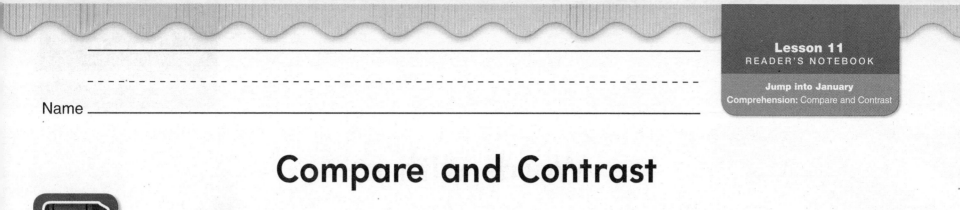

1. I can _____.

2. I can _____.

3.

Directions Read the sentences aloud with children and discuss how the two pictures are alike and different. Then have children draw a picture to show something they like to do in the summer or winter. Have them share their pictures.

Ask them to say where their pictures take place and use location words, such as *above* or *below*, to describe parts of their pictures.

70

Name _____

Sentence Parts: Subject

1. The dog chews a bone.

2. Sara sleeps.

3. The children like to slide.

4. _____

Directions Discuss the pictures with children and read each sentence aloud. Have children underline the naming part, or subject, in each sentence.

Then have children write a complete sentence. Have them share their sentences with the class. Challenge the class to identify the subject in each sentence.

Grammar

Kindergarten, Unit 3

Name _____

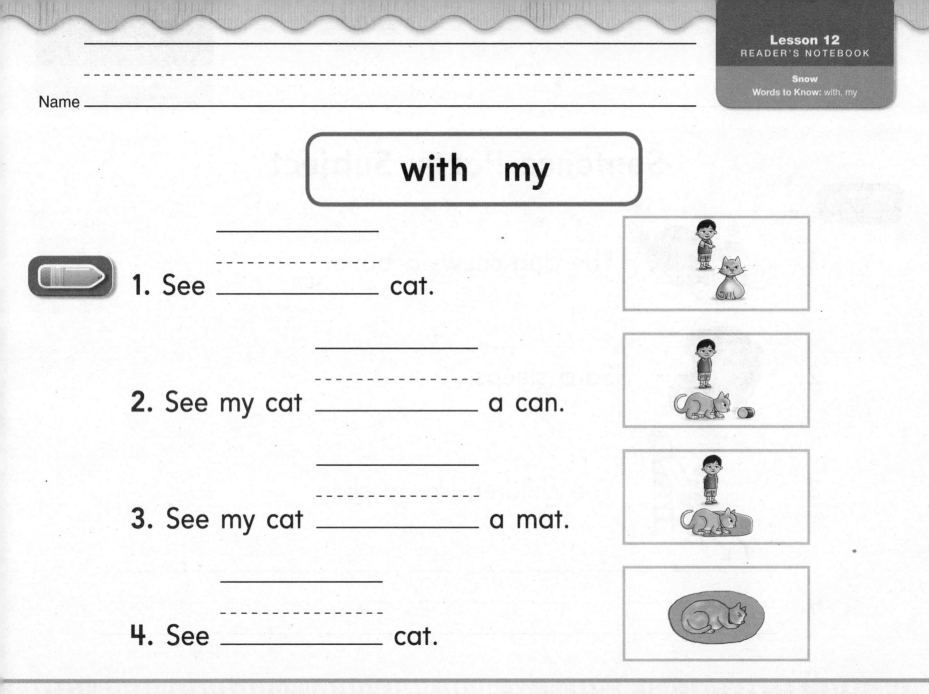

with   my

1. See _____ cat.

2. See my cat _____ a can.

3. See my cat _____ a mat.

4. See _____ cat.

Directions Have children read the words in the box and look at each picture. Then have them write the word *with* or *my* to complete each sentence. Have children read the completed sentences aloud.

Have children point to and say the names of the letters they recognize on the page. Then have children tap their desks once for each word as they read the sentences aloud again. Have children say other sentences with the words *with* and *my*.

Name _____

1. n Nn   N   n

2.

Directions Have children write their name at the top of the page. Have them name the Alphafriend and its letter. Then have children trace and write *N* and *n*. Next, help children identify the pictures.

Have children write *Nn* next to the pictures whose names start with the /n/ sound. Help children think of groups of words that begin with the /n/ sound, for example, *Nan knits nightly*.

Phonics
© Houghton Mifflin Harcourt Publishing Company. All rights reserved.

Kindergarten, Unit 3

Name _____

Words with *n*

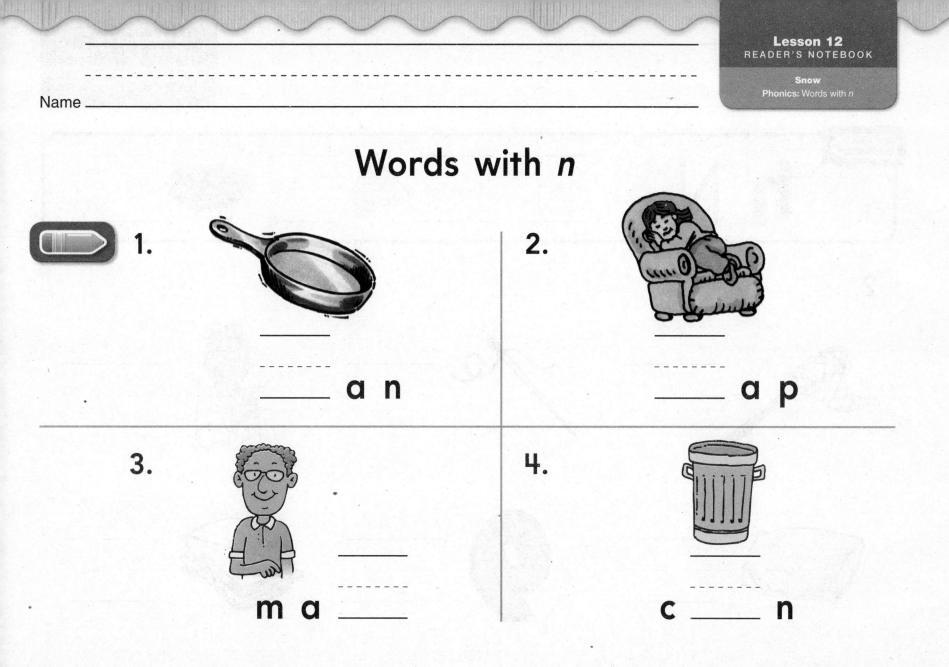

1. _____
   ____ a n

2. _____
   ____ a p

3. _____
   m a ____

4. _____
   c ____ n

Directions Tell children to look at the first picture and help them name it. Then have them write the missing letter to complete the picture's name. Repeat with the rest of the pictures and words.

Say pairs of rhyming and non-rhyming words that go with each picture. Have children raise their hand when they hear a pair of words that rhyme.

Name _____

Conclusions

Directions Have children look at the pictures and remind them what happened at the beginning of the story. Then have children illustrate how the bear feels when he hears the snow is coming. Have children share their pictures with the class.

Discuss with children how they used what they already knew and what they learned from the story when they drew their pictures.

Comprehension

75

Kindergarten, Unit 3

Name _____

Sentence Parts: Verb

1. The mouse rides a bike.

2. Josh builds a snowman.

3. The cat naps.

4. _____

Directions Discuss the pictures with children and read each sentence aloud. Have children underline the action part, or verb, in each sentence. Then have children write a complete sentence.

Have them share their sentences with the class. Challenge the class to identify the verb in each sentence.

Grammar

Kindergarten, Unit 3

Lesson 13
READER'S NOTEBOOK

What Do You Do With
a Tail Like This?
Words to Know: *you, what*

Name _____

you what.

1. _____ come with me.

2. _____ can we see?

3. We can see _____ and me!

Words to Know

Kindergarten, Unit 3

Name _____

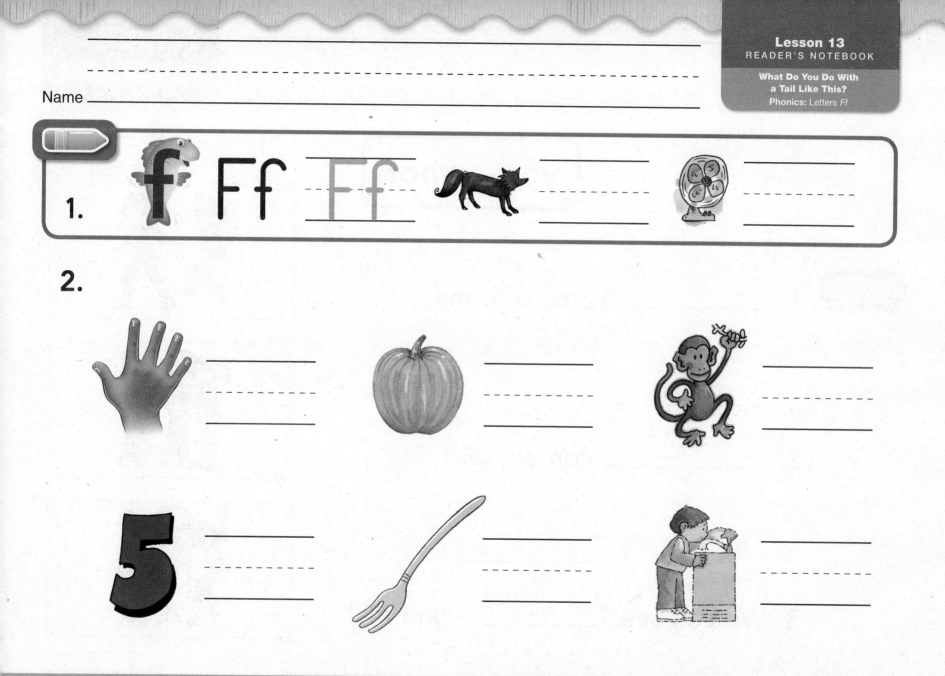

1. f   F f   F f   _____   _____

2.

_____   _____   _____

_____   _____   _____

Directions Have children write their name at the top of the page. Have them name the Alphafriend and its letter. Then have children trace and write *F* and *f*.

Next, help children identify the pictures. Have children write *Ff* next to the pictures whose names begin with the /f/ sound. Help children think of groups of words that begin with the /f/ sound, for example, *Four frogs fell far.*

Phonics
© Houghton Mifflin Harcourt Publishing Company. All rights reserved.

78

Kindergarten, Unit 3

Name _____

Words with *f*

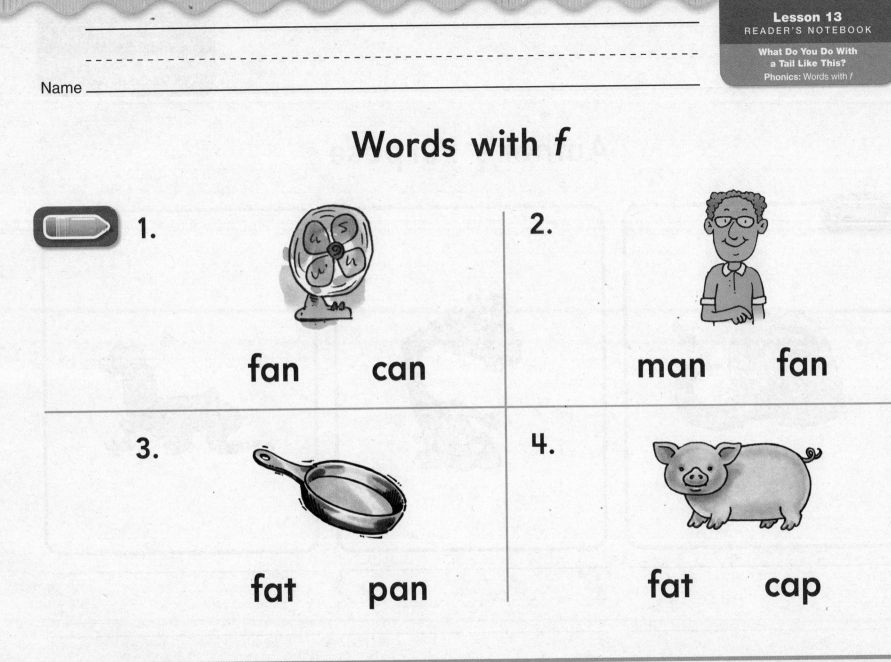

1.

fan   can

2.

man   fan

3.

fat   pan

4.

fat   cap

Directions Tell children to look at the first picture. Then have them circle the word that matches the picture. Repeat with the rest of the pictures and words.

Have children say the words that match each picture. Then have them think of words that rhyme with each one.

Lesson 13
READER'S NOTEBOOK

What Do You Do With a
Tail Like This?
Comprehension: Author's Purpose

Name _____

Author's Purpose

Directions Tell children to look at the pictures in the boxes and identify each one. Read the following sentence starter aloud and model how to complete it for box 1: *The author wanted me to know about___.* Have children do their best to write the response below the first box. Repeat for each remaining box. Then have children circle the animals for which the same body part was featured.

Comprehension

Kindergarten, Unit 3

Name _____

Complete Sentences

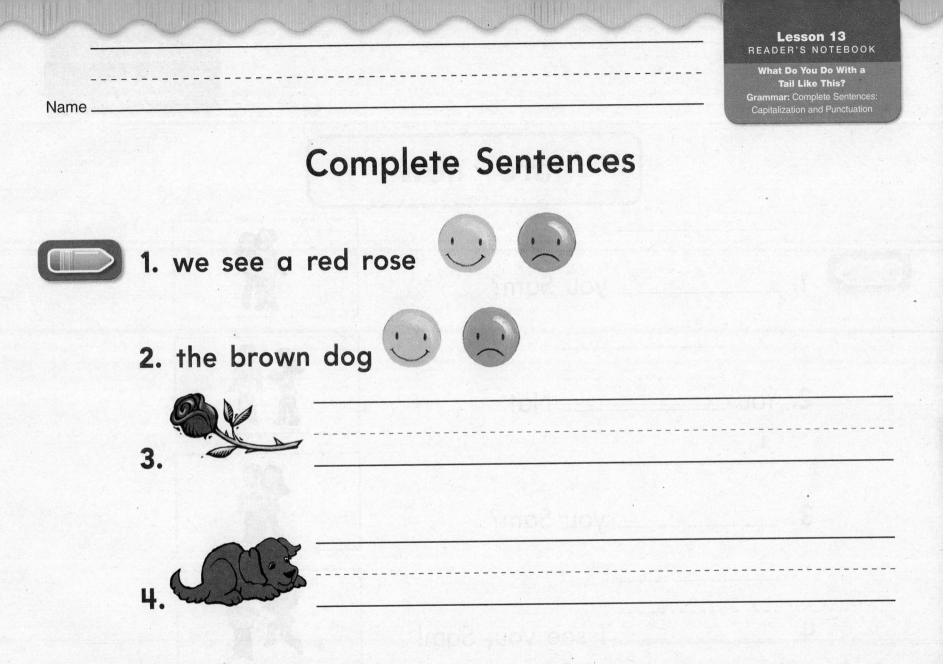

1. we see a red rose

2. the brown dog

3.

4.

Directions Read aloud the page with children. Have children circle the happy face if the words are a complete sentence and the sad face if they are not. Then help children make each sentence complete. As children rewrite each sentence, have them capitalize the first letter in the sentence and put a period at the end.

Grammar

Kindergarten, Unit 3

Name _____

are   now

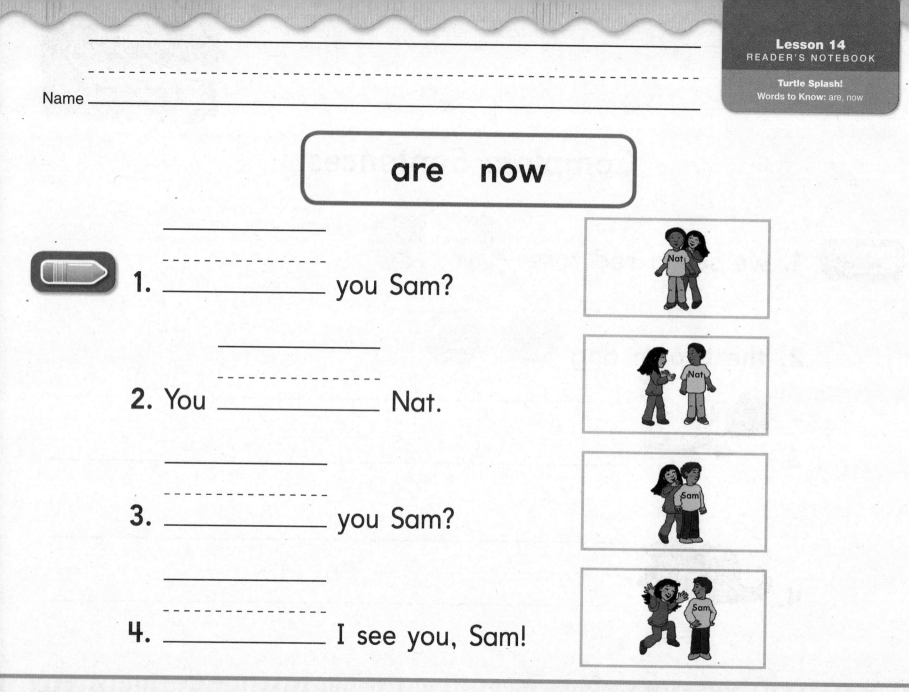

1. _____ you Sam?

2. You _____ Nat.

3. _____ you Sam?

4. _____ I see you, Sam!

Directions Have children read the words in the box and look at each picture. Then have them write the word *are* or *now* to complete each sentence. Guide children to capitalize the first letter at the beginning of a sentence. Then have children read the senten-ces aloud. Have children point to and say the names of the letters they recognize on the page. Then have children tap their desks once for each word as they read the sentences aloud again. Have children say other sentences with the words *are* and *now*.

Words to Know

82

Kindergarten, Unit 3

Name _____

1.

2.

Directions Have children write their name at the top of the page. Have them name the Alphafriend and its letter. Then have children trace and write *B* and *b*. Next, help children identify the pictures.

Have children write *Bb* next to the pictures whose names begin with the /b/ sound. Help children think of groups of words that begin with the /b/ sound, for example, *Busy blue birds blink.*

Phonics

Name _____

Words with *b*

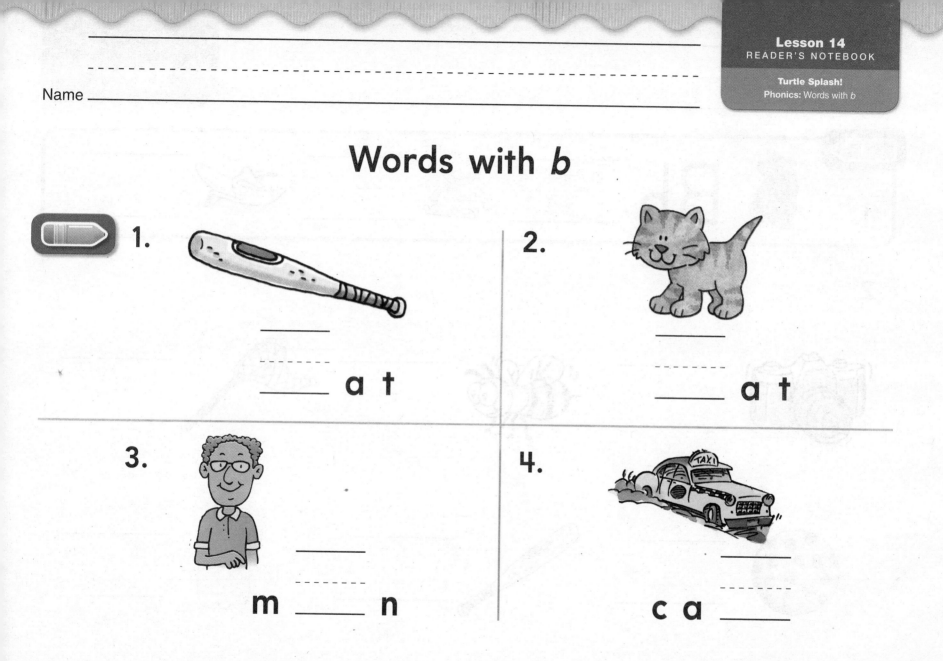

1.

_____ a t

2.

_____ a t

3.

m _____ n

4.

c a _____

Directions Tell children to look at the first picture and help them name it. Then have them write the missing letter to complete the picture's name. Repeat with the rest of the pictures and words.

Have children circle the words with *b*. Say pairs of rhyming and non-rhyming words that go with each picture. Have children raise their hand when they hear a pair of words that rhyme.

Phonics

84

Kindergarten, Unit 3

Name

Cause and Effect

Cause

Effect

Directions Have children look at the picture and discuss what is happening. Then have them draw a picture of the effect it has in the **Big Book** selection. Have children share their pictures with the class and tell about the key event in their pictures. Then have them tell about another cause and effect that happens in *Turtle Splash!*

Comprehension

Kindergarten, Unit 3

Name

Action Verbs in the Past Tense

I   We

1.

2.

Directions Have children name each picture. Then have them complete each sentence by writing a word from the box and circling the picture that shows what happened in the past.

Have children read their sentences aloud using a past-tense verb to describe the picture they circled. Tell them to speak clearly as they share their sentences and to listen carefully to others as they share.

Grammar

86

Kindergarten, Unit 3

Name _____

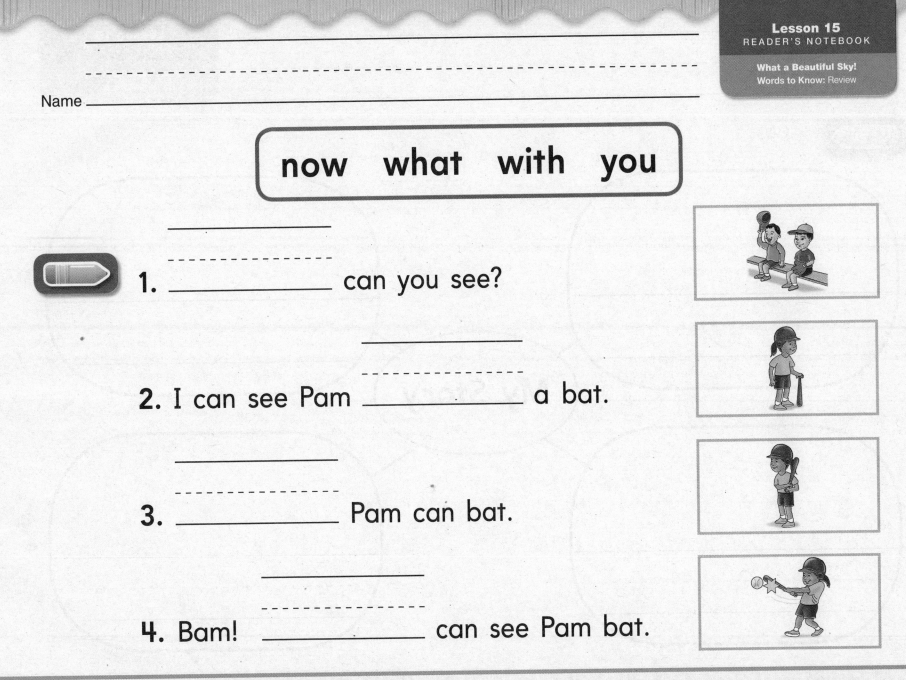

| now | what | with | you |

1. _____ can you see?

2. I can see Pam _____ a bat.

3. _____ Pam can bat.

4. Bam! _____ can see Pam bat.

Directions Have children read the words in the box and look at each picture. Then have them write the correct word from the box to complete each sentence. Guide children to capitalize the first letter at the beginning of a sentence. Then have children read the sentences aloud. Have children point to and say the names of letters they recognize on the page. Then have them tap their desks once for each word as they read the sentences aloud again. Have children tell a story using all of the Words to Know.

87

Words to Know

Kindergarten, Unit 3

Name _____

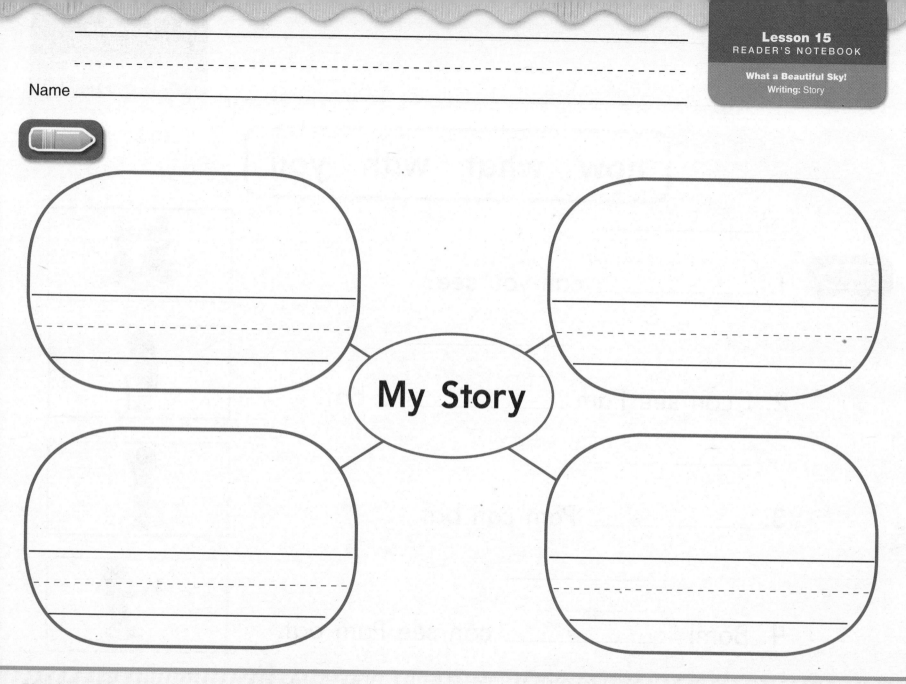

My Story

Directions Help children discuss and **generate ideas** for their own stories. Have children write ideas and draw pictures for their stories in the spaces in the graphic organizer. Guide children to write words or draw pictures showing the characters, setting, and what will happen in their stories.

Name _____

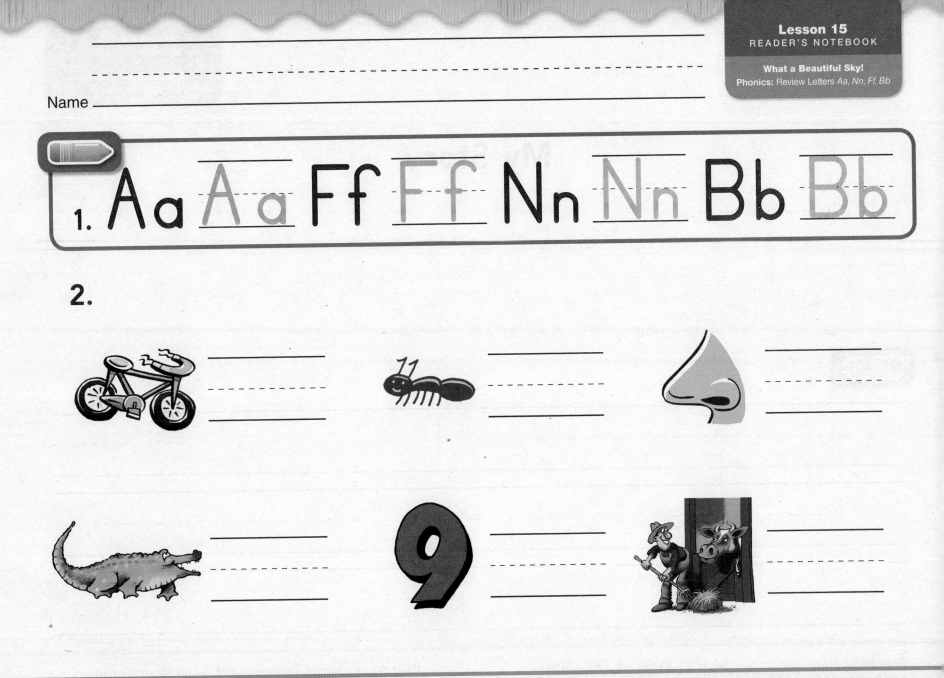

1. Aa Aa Ff Ff Nn Nn Bb Bb

2.

Directions Have children write their name at the top of the page. Have them name each letter. Then have them trace *Aa, Ff, Nn,* and *Bb*.

Tell children to name the pictures and write the upper- and lowercase letters for the sound they hear at the beginning of each name. Remind children to write the letters so they can be easily read, using a left-to-right and top-to-bottom progression.

89

Phonics

Name _____

My Story

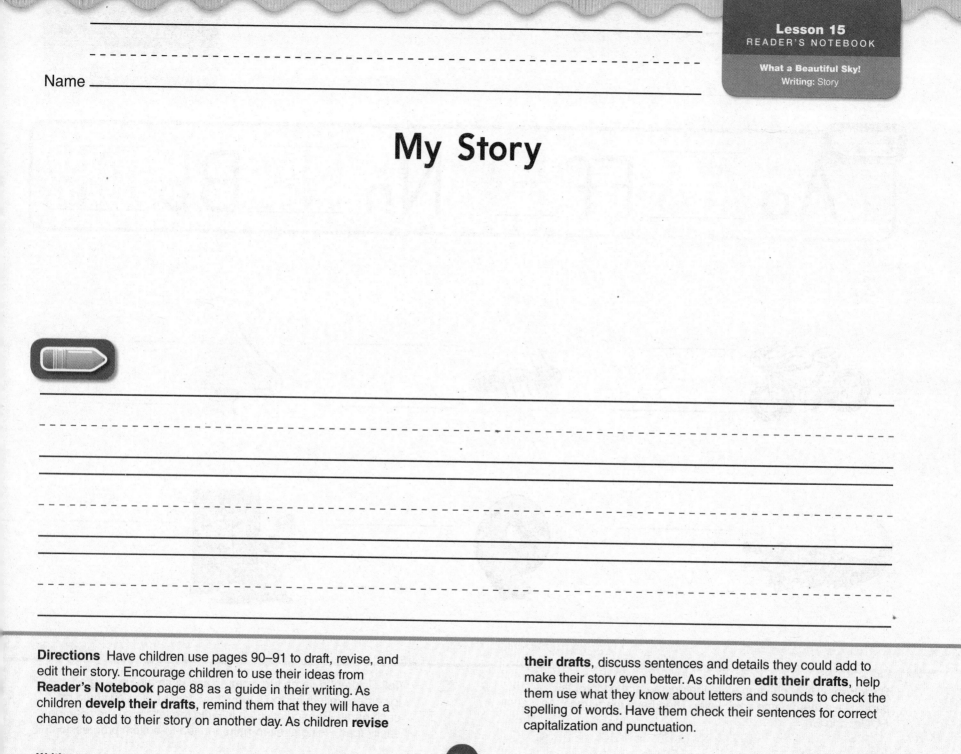

Directions Have children use pages 90–91 to draft, revise, and edit their story. Encourage children to use their ideas from **Reader's Notebook** page 88 as a guide in their writing. As children **develp their drafts**, remind them that they will have a chance to add to their story on another day. As children **revise** their **drafts**, discuss sentences and details they could add to make their story even better. As children **edit their drafts**, help them use what they know about letters and sounds to check the spelling of words. Have them check their sentences for correct capitalization and punctuation.

Name _____

My Story

_____

- -

_____

_____

- -

_____

_____

- -

_____

Directions Have children use pages 90–91 to draft, revise, and edit their story. Encourage children to use their ideas from **Reader's Notebook** page 88 as a guide in their writing. As children **develp their drafts**, remind them that they will have a chance to add to their story on another day. As children **revise their drafts**, discuss sentences and details they could add to make their story even better. As children **edit their drafts**, help them use what they know about letters and sounds to check the spelling of words. Have them check their sentences for correct capitalization and punctuation.

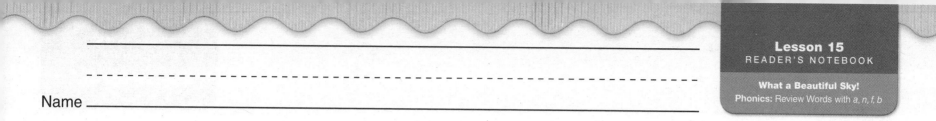

Name _____

Review Words with *a*, *n*, *f*, *b*

1.

cab   can

2.

pan   sat

3.

cat   bat

4.

fan   man

Directions Tell children to look at the first picture. Then have them circle the word that matches the picture. Repeat with the rest of the pictures and words.

Have children say the words that match each picture. Then have them think of words that rhyme with each one.

Name _____

Sequence of Events

Directions Have children look at the pictures. Discuss what the author tells about at the beginning of the selection. Then have children draw a picture of something the author tells about at the end of the selection. Have children share their pictures.

Have them use sequence words, such as *first, next,* and *last,* to retell the selection in the order in which the author tells about things in the sky.

Comprehension
© Houghton Mifflin Harcourt Publishing Company. All rights reserved.

Kindergarten, Unit 3

Name _____

Statements

1. the moon and stars

2. we see an airplane

3.  _____

4.  _____

Directions Read each statement aloud with children. Have children circle the happy face if the statement is complete and the sad face if it is not. Have children make each statement a complete sentence.

Then help children rewrite each statement correctly. Have them change the beginning letter of the first word to a capital letter and add a period to the end. Read the statements aloud with children.

Grammar

Kindergarten, Unit 3

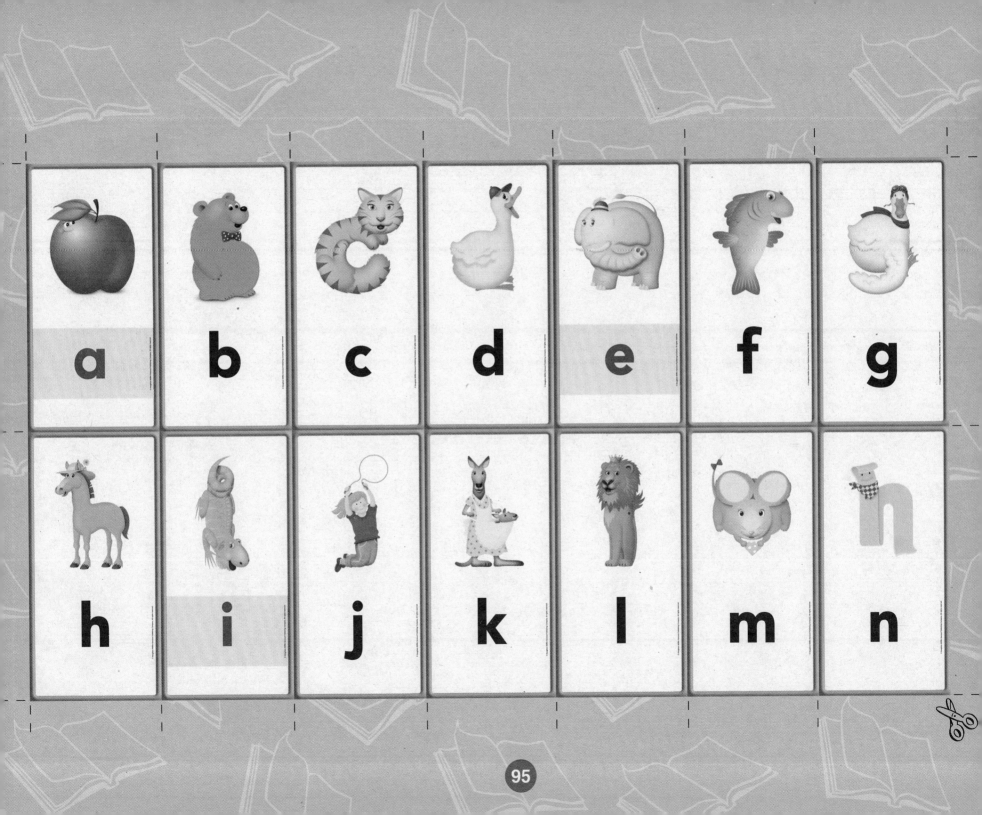

a
b
c
d
e
f
g
h
i
j
k
l
m
n

o p q r s t

u v w x y z

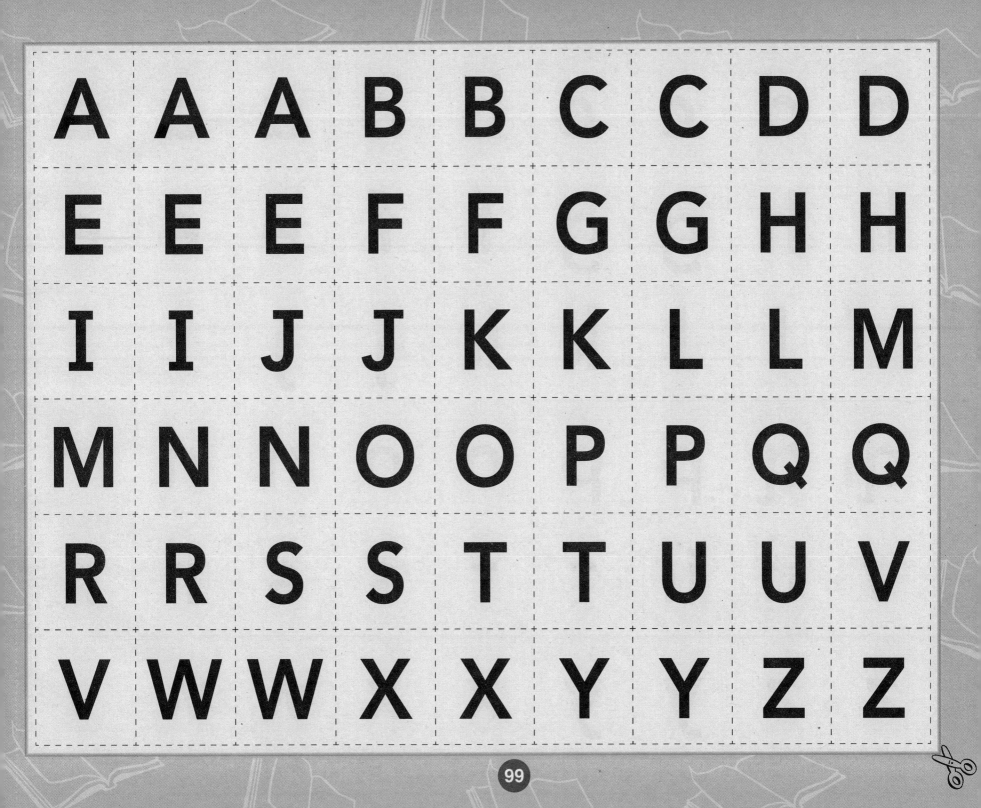

d	d	c	c	b	b	a	a	a
h	h	g	g	f	f	e	e	e
m	l	l	k	k	j	j	i	i
q	q	p	p	o	o	n	n	m
v	u	u	t	t	s	s	r	r
z	z	y	y	x	x	w	w	v

see

I

we

like

a

the

to

and

you	come
what	me
are	with
now	my